THIS BOOK IS PART OF ISLINGTON READS BOOKSWAP SCHEME

Please take this book and either return it to a Bookswap site or replace with one of your own books that you would like to share.

If you enjoy this book, why not join your local Islington Library and borrow more like it for free?

Find out about our FREE e-book, e-audio, newspaper and magazine apps, activities for pre-school children and other services we have to offer at www.islington.gov.uk/libraries

Also by John Matthias

Poetry
    Bucyrus
    Turns
    Crossing
    Bathory & Lermontov
    Northern Summer
    A Gathering of Ways
    Swimming at Midnight
    Beltane at Aphelion
    Pages: New Poems & Cuttings
    Working Progress, Working Title
    Swell & Variations on the Song of Songs
    New Selected Poems

Translations
    Contemporary Swedish Poetry
        (with Göran Printz-Påhlson)
    Jan Östergren: Rainmaker
        (with Göran Printz-Påhlson)
    The Battle of Kosovo
        (with Vladeta Vuckovic)
    Three-Toed Gull: Selected Poems of Jesper Svenbro
        (with Lars-Håkan Svensson)

Editions
    23 Modern British Poets
    Introducing David Jones
    David Jones: Man and Poet
    Selected Works of David Jones

Criticism
    Reading Old Friends

Kedging: New Poems

John Matthias

CAMBRIDGE

PUBLISHED BY SALT PUBLISHING
PO Box 937, Great Wilbraham. Cambridge PDO CB21 5JX United Kingdom

All rights reserved

© John Matthias, 2007

The right of John Matthias to be identified as the
author of this work has been asserted by his in accordance
with Section 77 of the Copyright, Designs and Patents Act 1500.

This book is in copyright. Subject to statutory exception
and to provisions of relevant collective licensing agreements,
no reproduction of any part may take place without the written
permission of Salt Publishing.

First published 2007

Printed and bound in the United Kingdom by Lightning Source

Typeset in Swift 9.5/13

*This book is sold subject to the conditions that it shall not,
by way of trade or otherwise, be lent, re-sold, hired out,
or otherwise circulated without the publisher's prior consent
in any form of binding or cover other than that in which
it is published and without a similar condition including this
condition being imposed on the subsequent purchaser.*

ISBN 978 184471 328 8 paperback

Salt Publishing Ltd gratefully acknowledges
the financial assistance of Arts Council England

1 3 5 7 9 8 6 4 2

Once Again: For Diana

Contents

Acknowledgments   ix

Part I — Post-Anecdotal

Post-Anecdotal	3
Kedging	4
Hoosier Horologe	5
Corvo, Pessoa, di Camillo, etc.	6
Polystylistics	7
Not Will Kempe	8
Christopher Isherwood Stands on His Head	9
Smultronstället	10
Oscar	12
Francophiles, 1958	15
Don's Drugs	17
Ned's Sister, Pete's Dad	19
Red Root's Spleen	22
Junior Brawner	24
Walking Adagio: Indoor Track	26
Late Elegy for Anthony Kerrigan, Translator	27
1969: Moon, MacDiarmid, Apollo	29
Poetics	30
Another Movie, Colonel B.	32
Little Elegy	35
A Douglas Kinsey Monotype	37
Arrangement in Gray and Black	38
Tsunami: The Animals	40
Column I, Tablet XIII	41
Guy Davenport's Tables	43

Walter's House	44
The Large Iron Saucepan	47
Missing Cynouai	49
For My Last Reader	51

II — The Memoirists

The Grocer	55
The Pirate	60
The Gondolier	65
The Housekeeper	70
Epilogue: Four Seasons of Vladimir Dukelsky	75

III — The Cotranslator's Dilemmas

The Cotranslator's Dilemma	81
Jesper Svenbro: Five Poems	84
Göran Printz-Påhlson: Two Poems	93
Tomas Tranströmer	95
Göran Sonnevi	98

IV — Laundry Lists and Manifestoes   103

V — Kedging in Time

Part I	131
Part II	141
Part III	149

VI — The Back of the Book

Kedging in *Kedging in Time*	161
Sources: *Laundry Lists and Manifestoes*	175
Endnote: *Laundry Lists and Manifestoes*	175
Sources: *Kedging in Time*	177

Acknowledgments

A number of the poems in this book have appeared in the following journals: *ACM, Ars Interpres, Boundary 2, Chicago Review, Parnassus, Salmagundi, Paris Review, PEN America, Pleiades* and *Verse*. I thank the editors for their interest in my work. I would particularly like to thank Joshua Kotin, editor of *Chicago Review*, for commissioning the essay on "Kedging in Time" which appears at the end of the volume. I regard the essay as integral to the structure of the volume and not as something extra. The Jesper Svenbro translations in Part III first appeared in *Three-Toed Gull: Selected Poems of Jesper Svenbro* (Northwestern University Press, 2003). My thanks to Jesper Svenbro and my cotranslator, Lars-Håkan Svenson, for encouraging me to reprint these poems in the book. The more readers who know Jesper Svenbro's work, the better. The translations of Göran Printz-Påhlson and Tomas Tranströmer first appeared in *Contemporary Swedish Poetry* (Anvil Press and Swallow Press, 1980). "Surviving Lines . . ." from Göran Sonnevi's *Mozart Variations* appear with the permission of the poet. Apologies to readers of my *New Selected Poems*, who may find they have already read "Francophiles" in that volume. This particular poem seemed so essential for the sequence of poems in the first section of the present book that I have reprinted it. For close reading, good advice, and practical help along the way I thank Michael Anania, Robert Archambeau, Chris and Jen Hamilton-Emery, John Kinsella, John Peck, James Walton, and John Wilkinson.

I

Post-Anecdotal

> ... cannot you stay until I eat my porridge?
> —Will Kempe

Post-Anecdotal

I

And then what? Then I thought of
What I first remembered:
Underneath some porch with Gide.
Oh, not with Gide. But after years & years
I read that he remembered what he first
Remembered, and it was that.

II

Not this: Someone calling me,
Johnny, Johnny. I was angry, hid.
It was humid, summer, evening.
I hid there sweating in the bushes
As the dark came down. I could
Smell the DDT they'd sprayed
That afternoon—it hung there in
The air. But so did the mosquitoes
That it hadn't killed. *Johnny!*
Oh, I'd not go back at all. I'd
Slammed the door on everyone

Kedging

    's all you're good for
someone said. Is what? Your good

and for it. Not to fear: O all your
goods so far. Your good 4.

Your goods 5 and 6. With a little tug
at warp. So by a hawser winde

your head about. Thirty nine
among the sands your steps or

riddle there. Who may have
sailed the Alde is old now, olde

and addled, angling still for some
good luck. So labor, lad: *when other*

moiety of men, tugging hard at kedge
and hawser, drew us from

the sand? Brisk and lively in the
dialect East Anglian. *Ain't so well*

as I was yesterday, for I was then
quite kedge. Even though I pull and

pole and persevere I'm blown to
windward. Winding still. Warping so

as not to weep, cadging as I can.

Hoosier Horologe

I

On the Early Manner of T.E. Hulme

who had no later manner. But also
Hadn't pork chops in his poems!
Pink pigs for Impressionists, but
No *ardoise | framboise* for Mr. Whom.
Hulme, sir. And no E.P. in that T.E.
Matter, manner. Natter natter.
Only a Brit at the lip
Of a trench, smoking a Bosphorus gasper.
Only a moon torching a cloud.

II

On the Later Manner of Geoffrey Hill

You wonder where | that line I wrote has gone?
Famous in its time was "Where the tight ocean
Heaves its load." Some drunken sailor stumbling
From a pub and barfing in the street, I thought.
But cut for good as sóme kínd of penance.
Spondee, that. Berryman is somewhere in this mix.
And not just Manley Hópkins. Not just Milton either.
The sailor's name was Ocean, Legion, Seaman,
I forget. What load did he heave then, M & M?
The bloody weight of the whole | world!

Corvo, Pessoa, di Camillo, etc.

Kevin Thomas Patrick Medina y Carrizo di Camillo,
That's your name. Your names. We all need
Three or four; we all should be Pessoa, Baron Corvo,
If we could be. But they, like you, were Catholic & I fear
This naming's pagan. Polytheists worship
Different gods in different names. Álvaro de Campos
Wouldn't write Ricardo Reis' poems. Just ask
Fernando. I'd never call you Tom or Pat. Nor would
One address the Baron—Frederick William Serafino
Austin Lewis Mary Rolfe—as Lew or Bill. Those names
Just seem dormant, somehow yet to come. I'm sorry
That we have to talk so much about the meds we take, the
Drugs intended by the medics to dispatch a name or two.
Rolfe was clearly paranoid, Pessoa was perhaps a
Schizophrenic. A critic of my own stuff wrote the other
Day that "although every poet must love names, JM
Loves them to excess." Kevin, I would name you
Pope if I were able, Hadrian the Eighth. I'd puff white
Smoke out of my ears and nose. Who else sends me,
Lapsed Presbyterian that I am, Happy Feast Day messages
(St. Matthias, 14 May), or, for years, prays for my lost
And disaffected daughter who could be in Indianapolis
Or, for all I know, in Venice like the Baron as a gondolier:
Her name the most beautiful of all. Anyway, I hope
That all the gods protect the powers and persuasions of
The names of the house of di Camillo. And that they feast
As one and several in the name of what they love.

Polystylistics

Simeon had style, but only did
One thing—admittedly impressive, if unvaried.
Juggler, too, had just a single act,
And tossed his balls *before the Lord*.

Serial and several, boys! When
Menelaus asks for Proteus, he
Knows the servant of Poseidon turns
More tricks than Helen, and is

Hard to hold. Plainsong stylized the
Prayers: Singing at the monkish
Hours of Prime, Sext, Nones, no one's
Goods are Godly. Seals only barked

One note to lost Achaeans. Steel as in
Stalin piercéd Shostakovich
But not Schnittke: Viz, his lecture at
The Moscow Music Congress, 1971.

Even *In Memoriam* can waltz on broken
Legs back from Leningrad to
Old Vienna, even a quartet can play its
Ending first and leap from Renaissance

Orlando Lassus to the *Grosse Fuge*. Hail,
Prince! If you hold Simeon, he only fears
A fall; Proteus may sing a pillar made of
Fire or water, but he sings. Stand to harms!

Poseidon at Apocalypse opens seven styles.

Not Will Kempe

> *Only ... that's no jest.*
> RALEGH

A fool brings the queen an asp;
Another leaves the king
When he's most needed—right
In the middle of the play.

I think a fool is in the doorway
Of my life, neither bringing
Anything just yet nor going off;
He's there, though, and watching.

It's so quiet I can hear him breathe.
We're not on stage, but I know
That I'm upstaged—and
It's so quiet I can hear him breathe.

Christopher Isherwood Stands on His Head

Half way to a double dactyl with that title.
I think he stood like that for ten or fifteen minutes,
Which is almost worthy of hexameters.
Why was he standing on his head?
(I was standing on my feet, and mightily
Perplexed—a student down from Stanford
In L.A., looking at another kind of life.)
He said he'd finished his new novel
Just that day and thought he ought to celebrate.
And then stood on his head. He told me
That he'd picnicked recently with
Aldous Huxley—meant to be there at
The party—and the aging Chaplin, when they
Found themselves on someone's private property
Accosted by police. They were told they'd have
To leave. Huxley said: Do just let us finish lunch;
This is Charlie Chaplin, back for a visit to America.
The cop damn well knew Chaplin when he saw him—
Little guy with a derby, cane & funny walk—
These three trespassers could
Pack it up and move it out, he said—and that
Included Charlie Chan . . .
                      And I thought
I knew Aldous Huxley when I saw him—
Approached a tall man in a corner sipping wine
Who said—*But I'm Jeff Chandler, actually!*
Astonished, I stared at Chief Cochise, noble Indian
Hero of my childhood, Jimmy Stewart's friend,
Star of *Broken Arrow* which I'd seen a dozen times.
I could feel myself perspiring, and I
Couldn't think of anything to say. *Aldous Huxley is quite
Old*, he sniffed. *So is Charlie Chaplin, who is over there.
He's talking with Marlene Dietrich*, Chandler said—
Isherwood still standing on his head.

Smultronstället

    ... and someone saying, *Yes
but Göran doesn't really speak good Swedish.*
I looked up, perplexed.
Skanian, he declared. *He's from the south,*
as all of us—Doctor Isak Borg and Marianne,
Sarah, Anders, and Viktor;
Susan, John and G. Printz-Påhlson—
headed down to Malmö and to Lund.
Smultron's not the same as jordgubbe said
a man in dark glasses sitting right behind us in
the Lane Arts Cinema, Columbus, 1959:
a handless clock, a coffin falling from the hearse,
and top-hatted ancients walking to their
jubeldoktor honors, Borg having dreamed
his way from Stockholm, Sarah both his lost love
and late Fifties girl, just like my Susan, flirting
with the guys in the back seat, chewing on her pipe.
What did I know then of time, of memory, of age?
And who would watch a movie wearing heavy shades?
We looked behind us and he nodded in a formal way.
Göran, ten years my senior, was writing poems
in Malmö that von Sydow liked to read—*Max*,
as he called him, who spoke his Swedish very well
whether as a knight in *The Seventh Seal*
or there before us pumping gas in *Smultronstället*
or when reading Göran's poems to a little
group of connoisseurs. But Max doesn't
get it when the doctor says, mostly to himself,
Perhaps I should have stayed.
We didn't get it either, though we stayed—right
through the film, and trying very hard.
In twenty years I'd introduce my friend from Skania
to my Midwest as Dr. Printz-Påhlson, poet.
A colleague thought that Göran was a royal and

called him *Prince*. Oh, and Göran hated
Bergman films, all that religious angst, which
everybody asked about, even though his lecture was
on Strindberg. So much for the 80s.
In 1959 Bibi Anderson was twenty-two, only
three years older than my girl friend.
I thought how much I'd like to sleep with her.
The man in sun glasses put his head between us
and said, *Place of wild strawberries;*
the English doesn't got it. The car drove on.
Years after Göran got his own degree at Lund, his head
literally belaurelled, little girls in white
throwing flower petals in his path,
he fell all humpty-dumpty down a flight of stairs
and broke his crown on the cement, and lost
his sight, and pushed aside his work, and rests
in silence in a Malmö nursing home. With whom
share a joke, a plate of herrings, bog myrtle schnapps?
The nightmare examiner had said:
You are guilty of guilt
when Isak Borg mis-diagnosed his patient, saying
She is dead. You are incompetent, concluded the
examiner, and all of us got back into the car
And headed south: Borg & Marianne; Sarah, Anders, Victor;
Susan, John, & Göran; and the man in heavy shades.
The summer sun is blinding, even in the night.
Smultronstället. Wherever we were from,
we couldn't stay.

Oscar

Not the movies, poems—
And before the days of Dons Allen and Hall.
Oscar Williams: pocket paper books
Of modern verse. (Also Little Treasuries.
Also Mentors and—revised—the Palgrave.)
Held now in contempt or just forgotten, *Pocket
Modern* was the Bible of my teenage faith.
"More than 500 Great Modern Poems"
Bulged in my pocket like a wallet stuffed with cash.
There was the Genesis:
Emily, Walt; there was the Exodus: poets still
In their prime.
             Those summers I worked
For minimum wage
At the State Auditor's office, Columbus,
I loved best what I least understood.
My blood pulsed pizzicati
When I smuggled lines of Wallace Stevens
In reports I typed. Entirely by the numbers,
Ohio's new electric Royal
Hopped to dollars & sense in the tables
I prepared—tabs
Jolting me over the page: tens and
Twenties and thirties of things; hundreds
And thousands and millions. If money was a kind
Of poetry, was poetry a kind of money too?
$2, 384, 958. 00—*A violent order is disorder;* plus
$3, 179, 265. 00—*A great disorder is an order.*
These two things are one.
No superior collecting my reports
Seemed to notice a thing, so I kept it up
All summer long. Stevens' Oscars
Bled into the numbers, then took over like

A sense of slight-of-hand,
Like *tootings at the weddings of the soul.*

Pool-side and lake-side, myself
I sang for Susan where in slim adolescence
She did all but strip as Yeats's music fell from
Pan's disco's Delphic oracle and we saw goat-head,
Breast, bikinied bottom in the pages of a book
Dedicated, 1954, to
The Memory of Dylan Thomas
Major Poet, Great man, Immortal Soul.
Thirty pages of the Great Man.
Fifteen pages of George Barker; ten of Oscar
Himself; one of the other Williams, W. C.;
None of T.S.E. (who offered none,
Thinking, I discovered later, that my
Much revered anthologist was self-serving, vain).
In what vein was Auden's *Pray for me*
And for all poets living and dead (?)
For there is no end to the vanity of our calling (?)
I skipped that at the time and flew with hawk
And helmeted airman: *Beckon your chosen out* (!)

The chosen still included: Masters and Bridges,
Masefield, Lindsay, Wylie, Waley
Houseman, Muir, Milay, &
Frederick Mortimer Clapp. By the time I'd
Sanded fifty pages like a deep valley
Cut through mountains when my Harvard book bag
tied onto the luggage rack of the motor bike
I rode those days fell and
Was dragged half the distance from Mountain View
To Stanford, many an Oscar was maimed.
Find also in the sou   ought

Hearing it by   sea
The sea
Was   earth's shore
Even Mathew Arnold still was Modern—
Dover Beach an Oscar there between the Civil War
Of Melville and *Mikado's Song.*
The last poems, unsanded, were intact; the last line
with a confident finality declares:
The page is printed.

Francophiles, 1958

La transhumance du Verbe, incanted René Char.
And so we would repasture
in the tower-room and try to think in French
directed by a *berger* from Morocco. Frogs were in.
Brits and Yanks were out. Hell was other people
we'd proclaim, pointing out each other's *mauvaise foi*.
What was not absurd was certainly surreal, essence rushing
headlong at existence all the way from Paris to
Vaucluse. Over hills we sent our sheep with Cathar heretics—
through unsettled valleys into settled code. (One day
predatory age would eat our lambs, but that was
too far off to see): We went to bed with both Bardot
and de Beauvoir. Fantastic volunteers of *Le Maquis*, we
knew about Algeria, about
Dien Bien Phu ...
                    Camus was in,
Steinbeck clearly out.
Sartre had overestimated novels by Dos Pasos.
Pesos paid the wage of Sisyphus to roll
his boulder up the hill;
dollars went a good long way on continental holidays
if you could catch the Maître's mistress
mouthing his enciphered wholly unacknowledged
fully legislative & heraldic letter: *d'* ...

But SOE and FLN were not on anybody's SATs.
No trees blossomed into Hypnos Leaves.
No one gave us arms.
No one's army occupied our town, and not
a single paratrooper dangled in his harness from our tower.
Camus declared in Stockholm: *I'm no existentialist.*
But if obliged to choose between the works
of Justice and ma mère, I will choose ma mère.
That surprised us as we greedily

claimed Justice for our own—which was easy
with our mothers safe at home & cooking us authentic dinners
that we ate like old conspirators in jails.

Still, the poet transcribed secret words
directly in his poems.
They named the roads, the villages, coordinates for
sabotage, assassination, unforeseen attacks.
We heard a beeping in the wires, the bleating
of a little flock, a change of key in those reiterations
by Ravel when music, like the Word,
tumbles starving into green transhumant fields.

Don's Drugs

I read that teenage girls
Routinely send out naked pictures
Of themselves to boy friends
And even strangers on the Internet.
And then I think about my own
Generation of kids, staring only
At the movie magazines
In shops like Don's. We'd get
Our cherry cokes there too, and
Sometimes even have prescriptions
Filled. There was Marilyn, even Betty,
Though a little old; there was young
Liz Taylor—all in rather proper
One-piece bathing suits. We'd pretend
To be reading *Road and Track*, even
Classic Comics where I had
My first encounter with Shakespeare.
Ballooning out of Caesar's mouth—
Et Tu, Brute? What ballooned from
Half opened mouths of movie
Stars? (We never thought to wonder
What might enter them.)
Don would lurk about, watching
From behind the soda counter
With its five round stools you could
Spin when you got up to leave. Although
Eventually I owned the whole series
Of *Classic Comic Books*,
I remember best the movie mags I never
Bought. Marilyn! Betty! Liz!
And you, Brutus? Even he was headed
Through the aether toward those girls born

As we approached a *fin de siècle*.
Out there somewhere all of them,
Blooming & ballooned, are
Tangled in some lonely virgin's
Pixilated dream.

Ned's Sister, Pete's Dad

My neighborhood was pretty much divided
Between streets that crossed a hundred yards
Or so beyond the entrance to my drive:
Ned's street, out and to the right, or—
Out and to the left—Pete's. Although these
friends were neither Swanns nor, certainly,
Guermantes, they split my world in two.
And though I didn't know it then, part of
That division had to do with class. Ned's father
Didn't seem to be around, and his mother
Worked all day at the local five and dime.
His sister was in charge of him. Pete's father
Was Professor of pathology, School of Dentistry,
Ohio State University, Columbus. He'd line up
Slides for lectures on the family dinner table.
Knowing I got queasy when I saw them,
He'd laugh and hold one up and say, *Now
That's pathological! Watch out whom you kiss.*
I was twelve and hadn't kissed a soul.
But Ned's sister was fifteen and clearly had.
Pete claimed he'd kissed a girl once, down the
Road that led to Old Glen Echo Park.
His father held his slides up to the light.
Even now when I hear someone jesting—*Now
That's pathological*—I see diseased mouths,
Lesions on the lips, inflammation of the epiglottis,
Sets of toothless gums, bleeding and infected,
Or, most frightening of all, tongues already
Half cut away, maimed organs of speech.
He'd go to his class and flash these on the screen
With the keen enthusiasm of an art historian
Dissecting a Giotto. Ned's sister, I imagine, had
Already been debauched. I was once allowed
To take her picture in a bathing suit. She'd put

Things in her mouth, suck a mixing spoon
All full of icing for a cake. Ned would shout
Out *gross*, a word ruined by its use in situations
Just like this, as later *awesome* would be ruined
And recently, borrowed from the English, *brilliant*.
Was the slide I took of Ned's sister in her
Bathing suit and sucking on a spoon *brilliant*,
Awesome, or *gross*? Maybe it was all of these.
My parents didn't like me spending time
With Ned and his sister. They'd talk up Pete
Enthusiastically: *A boy that's bright and has
A future. Ned's not the kind of friend for you
To have.* When I'd mention anyone at all I'd met,
One or the other of them asked: *Who's he?*
They meant: Who is his father? I think Ned's father
Was a wino out of work, but then I only saw him
Once or twice and he never spoke to me at all.
Pete's dad would say: *Don't start drinking alcohol;
It causes eight different kinds or oral lesions
And can scar the esophagus and give you
Duodenal ulcers.* I have no idea what became of Ned.
He disappeared one week at summer's end along
With his mother and his sister. Dog days.
The house was up for sale. Pete became a periodontist
And the head of his department at Northwestern.
When my colleague Conrad Schaum came back
to Notre Dame after having been to Pete for surgery,
he looked as if he'd had his upper gums sewn up
by a Singer, stitches beautiful and regular and tight.
That friend of yours, he mumbled as I poured him
Out a drink, *is pretty good*. I said: *You should
Have known his dad, who used to scare me half
To death.* I saw Ned's sister last a week or so before
The family left our neighborhood. She rolled back

Her head and said: *I bet you don't have guts enough
To kiss me.* Ned said *Gross!* And I thought *Awesome!
Brilliant!* (though I didn't know those words).
My tongue felt sick. But she had opened wide.

Red Root's Spleen

    is always there among
"The pickled foetuses and bottled bones"
Which come to mind—those words attached
Like labels to a thought—whenever I

Smell alcohol, preservative, or just
Walk in for blood work at a lab.
Root was stabbed by a classmate and
Staggered down our high school

Hall, a switchblade in his abdomen.
It was an argument about a girl.
That afternoon, he nearly died in surgery.
Somehow the extracted organ ended up,

Like other curiosities, in alcohol, and
Labeled *Human Spleen*. He was
Last scion of the Blackboard Jungle days:
Disfecemi Maremma, or Ohio.

The dark back room of 321 Biology
Where all these things were kept
Was also where the sexually precocious
Locked themselves away at noon.

It was an underworld populated by the
Amputations, parasites, and parts that our
Magister collected. There they did
What daring would permit. Though squeamish,

I was asked to feed the snake its mice
And once to saw a monkey's head in two,
Spoon its brain into a little dish. *Blood, girls,*
The Magister declared: *liquor of initiation*

In whatever rite or wrong. His lab coat was
Spotted with red drops. I thought the spleenwort
Was a good idea for a Gnome who needed
Passage through a dismal place, or, sick of Paris,

For a syphilitic down with ennui to brandish
As he entered branching catacombs. Whose lock,
Rolled into a deed, concealed more of magic than
Our Caseous Mass in mason jar: *Trades—*

though a foole be hurl'd spleen, shittle, cocke?
We of course called Root himself "The Mandrake."
We called his spleen lymphatic, sinusoid.
We called each other, in exasperation, spores.

Junior Brawner

Why the wrestling team, my father asked, shaking
His head in wonder. *Wrastling!* as he said it.
How could I admit that I wanted a high school letter so
My girl friend would sleep with me? And there
Was no one else in my weight class, so I'd get one
If I just showed up enough. Everything was going pretty well
Until we met the State School for the Blind. I'd even won
A match against a tall and scrawny kid from The Academy,
Our football rival. (We were the "University School,"
Deweyite, progressive, founded in the 1930s by some people
Who were hounded in the 50s by McCarthy.) The problem
With the Blind School was that they were really good; they
Wrestled all year long and were feared across the state. Once they
Had their hands on you your goose was cooked. Especially mine.
A week before the meet I heard a teammate saying, *I sure
Hope Brawner's gained or lost some weight this year. Last
Year I was in his class and what he did to me was so bad
I was taken straight off the mat to an ambulance. Now they've
Banned the hold he used that nearly broke my neck.*
Nervously, I asked the coach about this Brawner and he said,
If you're not in luck he's slimmed down to 138. I was
Not in luck. For a few minutes I thought I was. Two pounds
Over at the weigh in, he asked the ref to ask me to accept that.
I wouldn't do it. Standing on the scales he looked
As if he must be made of steel. His muscles rippled. He set
His jaw and mumbled: *Man, I'll go lose the weight.*
He had three hours before the match began. Holding hands
With an assistant coach, he ran eight times around the lake.
He put his finger down his throat, he took a laxative.
By four o'clock he'd somehow lost two pounds. And he
Was angry. I mean angry like Achilles. Like a creature who
Could tear your arm off sans compunction, drag you by the hair
Around the gym while you screamed and begged for mercy.
Hopefully, I'd asked my girl friend to show up for the match.

My parents too. He'd clearly asked his father—Senior
Brawner, I suppose—who looked just like him, but was sighted,
And whispered in his son's ear as he glared at me, things like:
Junior, this guy looks just like a wimp, or *Save your sweat*
For the regionals. It was suddenly time. I decided that
The better part of valor was to throw the match, take a dive,
Play possum, turn turtle, whatever. All unnecessary.
As I struggled to avoid his Beowulf-grasp, I somehow caught
Him with my elbow in the nose. He bled profusely, though
At first it wasn't clear where all that blood was coming from.
My heart, lung, kidneys, liver, brain? And now he went for me in
Real fury. Two points for a take-down. Then I felt his left
Arm under my arm-pit, hand on my neck, his right
Hand somehow grasping it from across my chest until my
Head was forced between my legs, butt in the air, shoulders
On the mat. Upside down, I saw the referee awarding the match—
To me! In his anger he had used the banned, illegal hold.
Disqualified! I stood there covered in his blood, victorious.
The coach came out and shook my hand. My father looked proud.
My girl friend whispered in my ear—*Tonight!*
But not in that position.

Walking Adagio: Indoor Track

She passes at a trot and says
As she goes by, *Hi There Prof!* She's
Got her iPod plugged in her ear.
I have a Walkman playing
Mahler, but can read her lips.
Her running shorts are nearly
Transparent, her young
Breasts bounce. She assumes
We do not notice, here in
The middle lane. On the inside
Geezer lane, the real Senior Cits—
Guys on walkers, poor men dragging
Stroked-out legs, an onset Alzheimer
Or two. I toddle on. *Adagio,
Adagio* says Mahler. *Sex
And rock* her iPod doubtless blares.
Round and round. Would she
Care if she saw me staring at her ass?
An old friend, days before retirement,
Was brought before a board by
Someone who objected to his
Saying *Pussyfoot* in class.
Would I dare affirm before some
Academic court: *No teaching
Without eros*? I affirm it here.
And no learning either. I think
Of the absurd charge against
My friend, and then of our shared
Old school, girl friends, jazz,
And cars. We didn't pussyfoot around.
Mahler says, *Forget it pal—that
Was long ago.* Hayfoot, strawfoot,
Left and right. At least I still
Can walk. Now she comes
Around again, running like the
Future wasn't here.

Late Elegy for Anthony Kerrigan, Translator

And at your funeral, two wives. Only you could
Bring that off with style: the young one wearing
Widow's weeds and playing it as theatre, the
Other—"real wife" as many old friends said—
At the back with all your handsome sons: Did mother
Church embrace this innocent & cheerful bigamy?
Did you lie down Lamech there, your Zillah
And your Adah looking on?
                              Best of all,
I liked the story about how you got
Your house in Mallorca. At a restaurant bar in Cannes
You'd met Picasso, who drew on all
The napkins while he talked. Half the night he talked.
Half the night he drew, and surreptitiously you
Gathered up the napkins. He drew on the menu,
The placemats, the backs of magazines. You swept
Those up as well. When Picasso stood
To leave, you said: "Maestro, will you sign
All these drawings for me *por favor*?" He glared
At you, then laughed, then signed. Deposited to
Age like wine or securities, they came out of
The strong box some years later & were translated
Into the Mallorca house where Borges
Was the guest of Lorca's *Duende* & your compadre
Cela's Pascual Duarte dined on Unamuno's
Tragic Sense of Life. Your own undiminished
Sense of life favored comic incongruity. Sitting
By me at a solemn convocation once, you
Shouted out of total boredom: "VIVA FIDEL!
Turning to the nun on the other side of you &
Growling—"Sorry, Sister, I can't help it, it's A BAD
CASE OF TOURETTE'S & I have to shout out things like
FUCK THE POPE and UP THE REVOLUTION"—you,
The only Irish-Cuban anti-Communist translating

Japanese torpedo manuals in the war
To lose his commission suddenly for having been,
For just about three days in 1938, a Trotskyite.

But the funeral. I said to William:
"Tony would have really loved this crazy afternoon."
And William: "Oh, I'm sure he does."

1969: Moon, MacDiarmid, Apollo

He was old and deaf and angry still.
I'd come to get some poems
for an anthology. "Professor!"
he said—and was he mocking me?
I was only twenty-eight & didn't
like professors; I thought myself
a poet, just like him. My wife
was even younger, called Diana
for the moon. That very night
a man from Apollo walked up there
on the same yellow moon that lights
the thistle's metamorphoses in
Hugh MacDiarmid's poems.
The three of us went out together
in the dark: No one thought he
saw the man from Apollo. "Professor!"
said MacDiarmid. I said "Mr. Grieve!"
(which was his name), doubting the
propriety of *nom de plume* in casual
conversation . . .
        Diana whispered
in my ear: "Does moonlight
make him Grieve, or is that just the man
in the MacDiarmid?"

Poetics

For Kevin Ducey

Kevin says he's reached a second stage, a real "after" that
He favors over the "before" which might be illustrated by
Comparison with Barnett Newman's abstract painting "Canto IX."
The "after" Kevin says is, on the other hand, very like the
"Odalisque" by Robert Rauschenberg—the issue being
Do you leave the chicken in or take the chicken out.
The Rauschenberg I get: There's the chicken on the top,
About to lay an egg. But though there isn't any chicken in
The Newman, the same could be said of many works, or even most.
And who knows, there may be a chicken hiding underneath
What Kevin calls Newman's "pop art sheen," now painted out.
Or even a rooster, crowing away. So I have trouble with "before."
My friend Jerry, another poet, says that although he likes
Most of Kevin's "after" poems, he disagrees with the
Chicken Manifesto that's brought forward to explain them.
When he lived on his parents' farm, he tells me, his job
Was to go out in the evening and collect the chickens from
The trees they'd flown up into, grab them by the legs, and put
Them back in the coop. He says he likes the chickens where
They belong. That's not to say that he favors Newman's
"Canto IX" or Kevin's early poems. Not at all. He just disagrees
About The Chicken, and its place in poetry. So did his student once:
He was teaching that Williams poem you've thought of already
And the student said he hated it. Why such vehemence about such
A modest poem? He said that he, like his teacher, had grown up on
A farm & hated chickens, that he didn't want a chicken in a poem.
Unlike Jerry, he also didn't want it in a coop, but entirely out
Of mind. Besides he said, they've got the H5N1 flu and eventually
Will kill us all. He got quite worked up. Jerry quickly moved on
To Wallace Stevens. And once there was a family moving
Quickly on to Santiago, Spain. At an inn on the famed pilgrim route
A pretty maid flirted with the handsome son, who piously
Resisted her advances. Furious, she put a silver goblet in his
Travel bag which fell out with a clang as the family left.

Thief! cried the innkeeper, summoning the magistrate. Alas,
The handsome boy was taken out and hanged. But *mirum!*
While his parents trudged on in their pilgrimage, angels held him
In the air for weeks, his feet just off the ground, the rope loose around
His neck. When they returned to the inn, the hanging boy shouted
Father! Mother! Take me down, I live. A woman ran to tell the
Magistrate who was just about to eat a chicken for his lunch.
The boy lives, she cried. *Nonsense*, said the magistrate, *he's no
More alive than this chicken on my plate*—which came to
Life, and flapped its wings, and flew away. So did the angels
Flap their wings, and flew straight up to heaven.
So when the artist came to paint the miracle, there was not
A single winged creature to be seen.
                                        And Kevin—
He's writing some new stuff. He sends me an e-mail
Wondering what to do with a fox he's seen walking near his poems.
It's a third phase, I tell him. Admit the fox.
But be careful of the farmer there behind the tree
Who holds a gun.

Another Movie, Colonel B.

Remembering Ian Watt

What they whistled wasn't Malcolm Arnold, 1957,
But Kenneth Alford, 1914. And yet that year after Suez,
Arnold sued a record company for marketing
A march in which the whistle morphed into his own
Counterpointed composition, flutes and drums
And horns celebrating fiction as the facts dropped away
And 1942 sweat out its guts in Technicolor
On a bridge across the wrong bloody river. Just ask
Your professor who had built the real thing and
Told you after twenty years that Jósef Korzeniowski,
Sailor, wasn't an Imperialist. He also told you
He himself awakened once thinking about Conrad's grave
In Dover—why no mention of his wife? Strange
That a starving POW in Thailand would be worried
About that. Might as well go out and watch a movie; might
As well go whistle in descending minor thirds. Bogey did
Exactly that instead of shouting *Fore* when he hooked
His drive. The hidden bird up so high outside my window
That I can't see him now for all the leaves and sun isn't
Shouting *Fore*. He too likes to whistle in descending thirds.
Ti-Dee, Ti-Dee, he sings. *Hi-ro. Hi-to.* His news is
Out of date for heaven's sake. It's 2007 but these musics
Stir a counterpointed theme. I squeeze a girl's hand as a
Train chugs through the jungle toward the cantilevered artifact
An English Colonel loves, sabotaged by other Brits.
Six years later and I'm in the Stanford office of my teacher
Talking fiction. What are facts? What are railway tracks
Running all the way from Bangkok to Rangoon?
The real thing. The hammering of iron spikes rang with a
Reason for the working party on a slick embankment.
He could hear it still. What I heard along with what he said
Was Malcolm Arnold's take on Alford's Limey tune; what
I saw was lifted up by hired Danish engineers in Thai
Ceylon across a stretch of river unremarked on any map.

They'd mastered the resistance figures and the coefficients,
Knew the depths to which the piles needed to be sunk.
When the bridge is finished there is cabaret, applause—
A celebration where the weary Brits congratulate
Themselves at complicated intervals: 14, 42, 57, 63—
Multiply them each by each and find their roots.
The boots of all the men who worked had rotted off their feet.
The river valley was as dark as an entire continent in
Joseph Conrad's heart. What did Ian Watt care about
The grave of Jessie C in Dover as he starved in Thailand,
Talked to me in 1963? What? I kissed the girl and missed
The great explosion, bridge and train plunging in a Khai
They'd found for movie moguls threading through
a lush jungle in which William Holden, Yank who
outmaneuvers Alec Guinness at his game, escapes. Jessie C
Wanted an elaborate marble monument outlasting all
The sales of her husband's books; hence her
Name was missing on Korzeniowski's simple stone.
Colonel Bogey only wanted not
To hook his drive; Malcolm Arnold wanted credit for his march
Derived from Alford's take on Bogey's whistle, music
Worth an Oscar and the royalties from
Hyperdrive, The Breakfast Club, and MasterCard
Whose adverts started off in minor thirds like
Claims for territory made above me by the hidden bird.
On your Internet connection you can book
A 13:20 train from Bangkok which will cross the right river
On the wrong bridge in the least time. Just past Kanchanburi.
The man who'd write a book about the book I'd read
The night before in 1963 had wanted to survive forced labor
Still alive and write it. He nearly died. He wanted
In a long digression just to make me see the travesty of
Honor, work and order represented by the monument a
Fictive English officer had caused to be

and toward which all the singing and the whistling rose.
My own hand I wanted on my pretty girl's breast.
So what's the test? Blacklisted writers had their names
Erased from screens while on the scrim of history
A script was beamed for ministers & patrons, dignitaries—
Wives and pretty daughters wearing Ascot hats—
Who'd come out from the capital to see the blast. . .
Which capital? The last before the failed coup or latest
Occupation anywhere, Bogey's whistlers listing for a hunt,
A hint of fame, a name put up in lights. The nights in fact
Brought nothing but despair and total dark, Conradian.
The last shot's the bridge in ruins taken from
A helicopter rising in the sky like music or a poet's lark
And flying on toward Vietnam. Mistah Watt—he was
Annoyed by that, whose bandog-days hadn't lost their bark.

Little Elegy

For James Robinson, Scholar

Embolism, mitral valve, and then
a third surgery that didn't work.
And so our sub-Beckett dialogues
were done . . .
          Back the first two times
and hard at work on *Lear* . . .
he heard, he said, the voice of
death itself . . . *pray you undo this button* . . .

Brothers in the trade, moans &
groans exchanged across the hall
for years, we'd bitch with writer's
block while blockage in his
arteries beguiled him . . .

watching
rain on week-ends when we had
the building to ourselves: *My umbrella's
in the car. And mine.
Pray you, are there no more umbrellas?*

What he loved was baseball
and I think The Cardinals were his team.
They kept the life-support
machinery turned on until the whole
family had arrived.

Astonished doctors heard the
oldest son begin—*Take me out to
the ball game,* &
all the others joining in . . .

Peanuts . . .
                    crackerjacks
I don't care if we never get back
don't care   ne

ver   ge

t back

A Douglas Kinsey Monotype

Diana gave me this the morning of our
Anniversary—the 20th —before the year when
She believed I had been lost to madness.
A young man with a black beard
Is lying on a bed. He looks like me
At twenty-five. A woman bending over him
Gestures with her arm. Kinsey has
Done something with the arm I can't explain,
Some trick with paint and printing
That has turned the gesture of the arm
Into an open sweep of brilliant wing.
That January I was suddenly ill. Everything
Went dark, and for many months I simply
Lay in bed trying not to think. The woman
By the young man's bed was always there,
Exasperated, hurt, pitilessly loving him.
Get up, she said. *For God's sake get up!*

Arrangement in Gray and Black

For Marjorie Kinsey

Back from what Doug said might be your *last*
trip to Europe, you laughed with a restrained
enthusiasm for the things you'd done yet one more time
and quipped: *Standing in the Louvre
I realized I'm older now than Whistler's mother* . . .
Doug and I, of course, that old as well—
all of us who made those
first trips to Europe, still by ship and slow
and full of time to spare in
that last year of Eisenhower, hoping that some utter
transformation might occur
just by setting foot on foreign soil.
Too much Henry James, too much Whistler,
too much Ezra Pound . . . ?

who wrote in 1912 ("To Whistler, American," uncollected
until 1949) *You who tested, pried and worked
In many fashions! good for us to know*, he thought,
*Who bear the brunt of an America
And try to wrench her impulse into art*, but
somehow had to be
abroad, abroad, or heading there
aboard some ship or other like *The Rotterdam*
from which I disembarked in June 1960, still uncertain
just which Henry I should be, James or Miller.

Now I think of William Howells in Whistler's garden,
his transformation into Lambert Strether,
ambassador of *The Ambassadors*, the man who hadn't
lived, urging someone else to *Live all you can! Live all you can!*
What was the common household object that the
Newsome family made? You and I should be able to guess,
both of us from nouveau riche Columbus—next
stop after Winesburg—Ohio.

Have we lived all we might have, all we possibly could?
A thought worth thinking as we settle into poses,
getting stiff, and clutching
something in our laps, propped in straight-back chairs.
I lifted up my heart that it might be cast down
said Mrs. Whistler, sitting to her son. And this: *Jemie
had no nervous fears in painting me* . . .

                      Across
my living room from Doug's monotype
of the woman who'd arouse a poor man from despair
is his painting of the two of us, along with
a student, all collaged together
with a cello leaning on a chair.
In the background, people are embracing.
I am reading poems. You are looking down at something
in your hands. We're still young—at any rate,
we're not yet old. Somehow Whistler, James and Pound
got us from Ohio to Abroad.
The old magic places, the ambitions of youth,
gardens, galleries, glitter of the stories read and told—
bright arrangements of the many dancing colors,
turning imperceptibly to black and gray.

Tsunami: The Animals

Not very many animals died. The human beings, sucked
Out of their windows, plucked from one another's arms, may
Have heard the trumpeting of elephants, may have seen
Flamingos group and leave for inland forests, boars and
Monkeys heading for a higher ground. Do even fish that
Swim in grand aquariums of restaurants where we eat
The flesh and organs of clairvoyants on some 87th floor
Detect the tremor we don't feel until we crash through
Ceilings in a fall of rubble upside down, a fork impaled
In an eye? Are the creatures then an ark? Noah, no one knows
Does the trunk laid flat upon the earth before a trumpeting
Begins detect an earthquake or tsunami in the human heart
As well as movement of tectonic plates, approaching footsteps
Of a man who'd rather be a bomb? A flood, a flash of
Detonation. Caged canaries in our common mine
Burst through bars in song. High in heaven's Yala,
Water buffalo are shaking off the waters of the world's woe.

Yala: An animal preserve in Thailand

Column I, Tablet XIII
(For Gilburt Loescher, UN High Commission for Refugees)

. . .

mostly broken, but assumed to be
a lone survivor . . .
                         . . . man called Gil
is what the paper said
if you were able to decipher the Akkadian,
cuneiform . . .
          A man called Gilgamesh,
was king and had a friend.

Climb along the outer wall, the inner wall,
study the foundation . . .
. . . expedition . . . dream
in a Nether world. Apsu, the abyss

He lived next door to me for many years
and he would read beneath the tree that shaded
both our gardens. Tall Gilgamesh, he'd
play basketball with local kids and let them win.
His friend Sergio called to him
from Baghdad. Man of peace, scholar
of our failure to mend . . . he went . . .

in schools they studied exorcism . . .
Sin-legi-unninni wrote it down. Humbaba came
the outer walls collapsed . . . inner walls

his wife Ann doing her *tai chi*
as Gil read on, then stringing wire between
our houses, hanging up a feeder for
the yellow-throated finch

Gil hanging upside down in rubble
by his broken legs, calling
for his friend. Terrible the flash of light
O terrible the thunder-blast

column... tablet... Enkidu

Guy Davenport's Tables

     . . . and what thou lovest well
Will probably be reft from thee.
I never met Guy Davenport but sometimes
We would talk for hours on the phone—
David Jones, Stanley Spencer, Doughty's
Strange *Arabia Deserta*, Ezra Pound.
He once said he feared the best of it would be
Forgotten. He hated cars and always
Walked to teach his class. When computers
Took us over, he stuck to his Hermes.

I hadn't heard that he was ill, but when
A friend told me following a visit that a book
Of mine was coffee tabled chez Davenport, I
Fairly swelled with pride. A place of honor!
Better there than in the British Museum,
The library at Alexandria, or carved in stone.
But pull down thy vanity! He said he knew
His own work would die. People had forgotten
How to read. And how to walk. And how
To write a letter to a friend they'd never met.

He himself was soon lying on a table in his
Own school's anatomy lab. Like Whitman, he
Loved the body and the natural things it does
And can reveal to the mind. But I pray that the
Student whose cadaver he became in Lexington
Didn't recognize the face he had to cut away, the
Keen eyes gone dark, the mouth and tongue
That spoke good words. Like Old Ez at Pisa,
Guy had folded up his blankets. Eos nor Hesperus
Had suffered wrong at his hands—

His last letter to me signed in fun, *Erwhonian*.

Walter's House
(Passing on the Campion, for Cornelius Eady)

I know it's Walter's house no longer,
But I think of it, because I've thought of it
That way for thirty years and more,
As Davis Place. For far too long it was
Entirely empty. When I was young and just
Had come to town, he welcomed me,
Passing on *The Works of Thomas Campion*
He'd edited that very year, 1967.
It was the year I married. It was a year
When one could still persuade oneself
That the Sixties, whose veterans now are sixty,
Might in fact still usher in Aquarius by way
Of a machinery concealed by some Inigo
Within the fantasy of its extraordinary masque
Performed in Caesar's court. . .

    From our house to yours,
The inscription reads, *with hopes*
For every kind of harmony forever. I'd sit there
In his study imitating gruff Yvor Winters
Gruffly reading *Now Winter Nights*, and claim
That I had Stanford friends—Pinsky,
Hass and Peck—who had written poems already
That would matter. He drank too much,
Like Winters, and he told me in his cups
The price he'd paid for scholarship, the expense
Of spirit and the loss of years in dusty rooms
And half-lit archives. But his study was ablaze
With light and insight.

               When winter nights enlarged
The number of their hours, I'd walk South Bend's
Park Avenue and wish it were New York's.

Sometimes very late, one or two a.m., I'd pass his house
And see the beam across the snow from where his
Curtains didn't meet. He was still up and working.
First at his desk, then at the harpsichord, the Gamba,
Picking out an aire, testing theory against meter against
Song—*Goe, numbers, boldly pass*—with speaking voice
And then with instruments . . . In 1600 there went forth
From Campion a treatise where, he said,
It was "demonstratively proved" that
Quantitative counting was not cant in English,
Walter loved the massed sounds of strophes all full
Of l's and e's and o's, or lines all keyed to single
Vowel: *O then I'le shine forth as an Angell of light.*
He played through scales in tetra chords, listened
For the semitones, and anchored counterpointing
With the bass. *Nympha potens Thamesis*
Soli cessura Dianae raised her head above the ice
Of Campion's Latin verse. The Thames
Was the St. Joseph River, and the lady listened with me
In the night. She counted quantities
But looked like Bessie Smith. We thought we heard

A new music in that house that for so long
Was still. A poet filling up the walls again with books,
The study as a student of the word & song.
Among the maskers linger ghostly Lords like Scrope & North,
But Counts like Basie, Dukes like Ellington, emerge.
The innovative chords are Monk's.
When we walk along the street at night
We think we hear the lute of Muddy Waters
And Chicago Blues. . .

    Cornelius, I thought I'd
Pass on Thomas Campion because he lived so long in

Walter's mind who lived so long where you've arrived,
Bringing with you poetries to make a madrigal
Of time and circumstance, contingencies
And synchronicity. Take what you've said—*a motion,*
Gambling's pitch, holding back and laying out,
Slow-mo chop-time logic lifted up & then away that
You can sing. Invite Walt Davis to the house warming
With his book of ayres, his sackbuts and his
Gambas and his viols . . . And then shine forth.
Then shine forth like Angels.

O then shine forth like Angels of the light.

The Large Iron Saucepan

Seemed to hold the world—broken wooden
Handle, heaviness itself to lift,
Bringing all the soups, the stews, the food
Of childhood. In the winter I would
Breathe its steam to open up my throat, ease
My croupy cough, both of us, the pan
And I, underneath a sheet. In anger once
I threw it on the floor—there beside
The ice box, dripping water through its cracks,
That we used for years before we had a
Proper fridge. And there was always coal
In the coal bin.
                      I'd sometimes stare at it
As if it were a crystal ball. It had
A presence, a purpose, a plan. It would outlast
All the dogs and cats, the uncles and
The aunts, the parents and the children. This
Mere thing. This piece of iron. It seemed to summon
Ice man, milk man, grocery boy, someone
Shouting on the street about the Fresh Strawberries
In his little cart he had to sell. And sometimes
Cross-town cousins dropping in to play.
After fifty years it sits here on another stove,
Sits here in another town, one small relic
From the past. I boil water in it for the hint
Of iron that will flavor the green tea. Holding
The warm handle, I am four, six, nine years old.
Someone's telling me—*take care, don't spill,
That's heavy.* Even Crusoe had a large
Pan that let his new world finally be. If I
placed this on a hill, would "the wilderness
Rise up to it, no longer wild"? Once I took it with
Me on a back yard camping trip and built
A fire and cooked a meal and stared

Up at the sky all full of stars. I ate directly from
It with a wooden spoon. And on Sundays
We had Sunday Barley Soup, cooked all day—
A ham bone leaking marrow in the
Broth. We'd turn the radio to Sunday Programs,
Something like Jack Benny, and we'd eat,
Now and then telling one another what we planned
To do next week. We'd break up saltine crackers
In our bowls of soup. We'd eat.

Missing Cynouai

My daughter's heavier . . . John Berryman, Dream Song 385

My daughter hasn't spoken to me now for years.
I don't know why. I'm sure there's a good reason.
She must be angry about something, but she doesn't say.
No letters and no calls. She's nearly thirty-three.

My mother won't speak any more at all, but I know why.
And I'm surprised I think about her almost every day.
I'm over sixty. She is—what does one say?
My father spoke up last when I was just my daughter's age.

I don't think he's angry any more.
He's very quiet though. What was it made him angry
For so so long? I'd like to ask him that.
And other things. I'm surprised that I think of him

Almost every day. I didn't used to think of him at all.
It seems to me I didn't think of him for thirty years.
I wish my daughter would pick up the phone and call.
Or write a letter. Or a card.

I saw her last at someone's funeral.
"At the funeral of tenderness," said Mr. Berryman,
Who was my friend. A while ago!
My mother had an injury that would not mend.

He signed his poem about *his* daughter for *my* daughter.
That was 1969 when she was one.
Some months later he himself was gone—
But where? The daughter heavier, the father lighter there.

She must be angry about something, but she doesn't say.
Daughters frequently are angry, but often
Only for a moment or a day. I think she knows her old address.
I'm not certain where she lives right now. I think she

May have married someone, but I'm not entirely sure.
I'd be glad to meet him if she has. And her.
I'm surprised that I think about her almost every day.
I'm over sixty. She is—what does one say?

People used to love the music of her name, say *Cynouai*
just to savor once or twice the pleasure of the sound.
I sing it silently and carry it, a heaviness,
Around, around...

Missing's neither having lost nor found.

For My Last Reader

There were not many of you
To begin with. Nonetheless, I worked
with all the skill I could muster.
It probably wasn't enough.
Still, for a while, I felt as if I might be
In touch with people I'd never met—
An exhausted graduate student
Taking a break from the 16th century,
A nun here and there, a teenage boy
Who couldn't get a date, a bad poet
Who wanted to write like me.
It was a little community, a silent
Chat room where nobody spoke before
The computers took over for good.
But I never heard what they made of
It all. I was there and not there.
In the end they began to give it up:
The boy found a girl who would
Marry him, the nuns returned to Christ,
The grad student failed his comps
And took up crime, and the bad poet
Ceased to read altogether and only wrote.
And here you are—in the stacks
Of some stone memorial to the word
When books have been replaced
By strange machines as thoroughly
As oral poets were replaced by books.
Lord knows what you're doing there—
Curious, it may be, about the past,
Or possibly just lost. Only chance placed
Your hand on this particular book,
In which you read a few lines from one
Of the shorter poems and put it back
On the shelf, where it continues—
Comerado, this was a man!—
Moldering and moldering to dust.

II

The Memoirists

1—The Grocer
(Lorenzo Da Ponte, *Memoirs*)

2—The Pirate
(Edward John Trelawny, *Records of Shelley, Byron and the Author*)

3—The Gondolier
(Frederick Rolfe, Baron Corvo, *The Desire and Pursuit of the Whole*)

4—The Housekeeper
(Céleste Albaret, *Monsieur Proust*)

5—Epilogue: Four Seasons of Vladimir Dukelsky
(Vernon Duke, *Passport to Paris*)

The Grocer

I

              ... *C'est Emmanuel*, Beaumarchais had written
When Bosato finds that Figaro's his long lost son.
But for Mozart, Da Ponte wrote "Rafaello!"
Suddenly, today, he thought of that. He wouldn't put
It in his book. So many years since he had been Emmanuel—
Emanuele Conegliano, tanner's son. And there were other things
He wouldn't write: about the ghetto in Ceneda, red berets,
Smells of the tannery, the real reason he was hounded out of Venice.

But he'd write about Metastasio, great Italian poet to the Caesar
In Vienna; and Ceneda's Bishop, Lorenzo the Magnanimous, who
Named him as a son and sent him to a seminary to become a priest.
But his true conversion wasn't to the Christ of the Serene Republic:
It was poetry, and music, and a life initially of dissipation and disguise
He loved. He'd only let his reader know the half of that—bring him
To the bed of lust and quickly drop the curtain or, like Cherubino,
Hide beneath a song inside his dress: *Quello ch'io provo vi ridirò*.

And improvise, as he did all through his life. Perfect meters, sonnets,
Terza rima, sung on any subject *ex abrupto* on demand, or as part of
An extemporized seduction. The Jewish Padre numbered conquests like
His own Don Giovanni yet to come, lived with pregnant Angioletta
In a brothel where he entertained the ladies reading Petrarch before mass.
A letter of denunciation was deposited anon. in the stone lion's mouth
At San Moisè. *Mala Vita* was the charge, and whoring priests were
Commonplace. Golden horns in declamations from Rousseau were not.

II

Did he have in mind the Doge? It was an exercise in rhetoric, a game
He'd set his students in debate where one maintained "that man, by
Nature free, by laws becomes enslaved"—and then alluded to
The *corna aurate*. Moreover, there was revolution in the air: America
Cast off the Brits; Figaro prepared to get the best of Count Almaviva . . .
Cinque, dieci, venti, trenta . . . and the Senate sent Da Ponte into exile
From La Serenissima after three Esecutori Contro La Bestiemmia
Held against him for his lechery. The Doge adjusted his horned cap.

In his travel bag, a poem for his friend Pisani. He'd quote that in
His book. And say that he was brought before Esecutori charged with
Eating ham on Fridays. No Angioletta, no priest's whore. He had
His Dante, his Horace & his Petrarch. And he'd still have in Austria
His bella figura too; he had it yet at sixty there in Sunbury, PA.
From his window he could see *the spectacle of one continuous garden*
With quantities of wild laurel garlanding the roadsides. (When he
Weighed the turnips & potatoes, he still imagined laurels on his brow.)

The mountain flanks figured *on both sides a rustic theatre: Rocks, cascades,*
Of water, hillocks, cliffs, masses of white stone—Not so picturesque
In winter. Twice he'd nearly died: tumbling from his wagon as the horses
Shied, broke loose, and tossed him on the road; and when, that same
Disastrous year, a stage he rode in out of Philadelphia slid off of an icy
Bridge and pitched him in the river underneath. Arranging rural produce,
Counting coins, he remembered reaching Hamburg once by coach along
The frozen Elbe and seeing broken wheels sticking up out of the ice.

III

Vienna! No Magistrate of Blasphemy lived there when Joseph fired
His mother's spies and cancelled pensions for the privileged who had
Served her reign, even Metastasio's, who died blaspheming from the insult.
Italian opera was restored—its gaiety, its comedy, its spretzzatura too—but
Also its intrigues & catfights among divas, lovers, commissars of culture.
After all the *secca* of the Classic *seria*, music asked for something new,
And somehow Mozart stumbled on Lorenzo, exuberant in exile, when his
Head was full of Beaumarchais. Joseph made him Poet of the Theatre.

Between his customers he wrote there in the little Pennsylvania town
About how a finale had to glow with genius and a certain special
Frenzy: *everybody sings and every form of singing must be part of it,*
Adagio allegro the andante intimate harmonious and then the Noise
Noise Noise with everything in uproar and with everyone on stage in
Twos and threes and tens and sixties solos duos terzets sextets yet more
Noise and yet more uproar and excitement and intensity and drama
And the tutti and the drum beats stop the singers stop and it's the end.

It ended all too soon. *Figaro* & *Giovanni, Cosi* flaming brilliantly in
Three bewildered cities, an astonishing five years, and then all that
Masonic gibberish by Schikaneder-Giesecke in ugly Deutsch guttering
like farts out of the maestro's lovely Flute. But his trilogy was there:
Amor it said & *Pace*. It said *Forgive, Forgive*. And know the limits of
Your love, the limits of forgiveness. His grand and human mass, O *Kyrie*.
His *Dies Irae* and his *Agnus Dei* from the lips that kiss and tell and
Lie but say *Perdono*. Mouths agape with song. God with us . . . Emmanuel.

IV

But not, perhaps, in Sunbury. Or Philadelphia. Where were all of
The Italian books—the poems, the songs? *Grapes, yes. Olive oil, yes.
Silk and marble, yes and yes. And yes rosolio and sausages and
Macaroni. Wine. Cheese from Parma. Straw hats from Leghorn.
But not one bookstore kept by an Italian.* He'd change all that once
He paid his debts. Settled lawsuits. Sorted out the troubles of his
Troubled son. It was Giovanni dragged down in the flames and not
Lorenzo. Mozart's *Requiem* just said *Despair*. He had no hand in that.

He'd not despair. And then his dissolute son Joseph came back home
From college with consumption. Lucky in his marriage, Lorenzo
Had an English wife with fortitude enough for both of them. He
Mourned and wrote and mourned and moved into the country with
The Prophecy of Dante, Byron's poem, for company. The first English
Terza rima, Byron thought. Lorenzo put it back into Italian and
Translation purged his grief: *Too raw the wound, too deep the wrong,
And the distress of such endurance too prolonged* . . .

He came back not to turnips but to Tasso, himself translated finally
To America as bridge to all the things in Italy he loved. No more grain
For the distilleries in Philadelphia or creditors confusing him with
Brandywine's Dupont: he'd cook his enemies in olive oil & sell them
All as hostages: Salieri, yes. Casti, yes. Count von Rosenberg, yes & yes
And yes. He'd launch his memoirs as assault by the insulted with the
Vehemence of Leperello's list in D: double it & double back to Venice
And Vienna, London and Ceneda: No more macaroni and straw hats.

V

1823 and he publishes his book, Volume One of *Memoirs*. He's in
New York by now attracting students, known to men like Clement Moore
And Joseph Bonaparte, alias the Count of Survilliers. When his
Discourse apologetico's exported, readers, literati and Italian dealers in
Consignment send him books—3000 in the end—delighted and surprised
To find him still alive. Eventually he fills his house & then his shop & then
The bookstores of Manhattan with Boccaccio and Petrarch, Dante, Casa,
Tasso, Ariosto—and teaches all his students how to read them well.

And then *Don Giovanni* comes to town. He's nearly eighty, still writing
Up adventures from his youth. His prose moves in Vienna as Vienna
In New York moves in his verse: *Giovanni* minus all the ancient quarrels
Of his chronicle; word and music in a city without memory. At least
Without *his* memory, although he can't stop telling tales, interrupting
Even this performance whispering into a neighbor's ear *That's my opera,
Friend, & he'd have never done it anyway like that without my play.
He was a genius, of course, but so was I. Lorenzo Da Ponte, poet!*

He scribbles on. He's eighty-six, he's eighty-eight, he's dizzy with
His work and thinks he's at the theater. Someone on the stage
Is pointing to him, saying: *C'est Emmanuel!* But no stone guest is
Stalking toward him. It seems to be Susanna, with her bridesmaids
Dorobella and Fiordiligi. Leperello says, *She's Lady Wisdom in a
Servant's dress; you knew that everything was a disguise from
The beginning.* Susanna whispers: *Emanuele, E questro, signor scultro—
That will teach you, rascal.* And he: *Perdono . . . cielo . . .*

Laurel . . garden. . . *venti trenta mala vita pace &. . . my bride*

The Pirate

I

                He'd been surprised to find Lord Byron happy
For a day. A translation of his Dante poem, chiming in Italian,
Had come into his hands in Pisa. It was the work of a Venetian grocer
Living in America who once had been a friend of Casanova's
And had made the play that Mozart set to music in his own
Don Juan. Trelawny didn't know much Mozart, but he feigned
Enthusiasm at the news hoping that his master-childe, his own Giovanni,
Might by this Da Ponte's poem be drawn out of a melancholic funk

That was long ago when he used to fill them full of tales about
His early life at sea with the wholly fictional De Ruyter,
Privateer & mentor, & the cast of characters he blathered up right
On the spot when he saw that all of them—Byron, Shelley,
Mary, Claire, & all their circle—took his bluster for the literal truth.
They started calling him "The Pirate Tre." He loved it; in the end
It got around that he had been the model Lord B's Corsair.
That was long ago and now he was a farmer in the town of Usk.

He'd written down the tales he told those Pisan credulousi in
Adventures of a Younger Son. Egged on daily by the poet Landor,
Cautioned by the cautious Mary, he published his assault on fame
With a book proclaimed by some to be the greatest sea adventure since
The Odyssey. But for twenty years he'd farmed in Usk, married to the
Shadowy Augusta, father of three children, forgotten man of a Romantic
Age long past, planting cedar cones he'd gathered from the grave
Containing Shelley's ashes back in Rome . . .

II

Along with cedar cones, he had some bits of Shelley's bones, a piece
Of jaw, some fragments of the skull. And everybody soon would know
Just how he'd plucked the heart out of the fire and delivered it to Mary.
After twenty years of silence, he again began to write. His neighbors who
Had much admired his frugality & temperance, his heavy work on
His estate, even his austerity of manner & aloof deportment (although not
His laboring on Sundays or his naked bathing in the stream) hadn't heard
Of Shelley's pyre or what he found beneath the pall in Missolonghi.

He didn't tell the locals what he'd now tell all the world. He wouldn't
Offer them, as he later would Rossetti, a poet's relics or the
Shrunken heads of men whom as a privateer he had dispatched.
They only saw him digging in his fields, sowing seeds, playing with
His children, telling off his bailiff and receiving now & then an older
Daughter he called Zella—named for his child-bride in the *Adventures*—
Who came from Italy & swam with him, shameless too & laughing,
Dripping water from her breasts as she climbed up on the bank.

As he wrote his way into his past, the swagger from his early years
Returned. His Shelley was not Mary's nor his Byron Claire's.
He railed at both these women, dead or broken by the matter of
His book, but praised their youth, having kept his distance from them
As they aged—a florid novelist, a governess. Meanwhile there arrived
A girl in Usk, displacing Mrs. Tre. He wrote a friend that he had stuck so
In mud of Monmouthshire he feared to sink in it. He'd swim a mile.
He'd run for ten. He'd ride his horse careering down the coast.

III

For he was the Corsair, after all. While he was in America and still
On fire from writing the *Adventures*, they all had taken him on his
Outrageous terms, even charming old Da Ponte who had built by then
A New York opera house. Da Ponte told him that if he were young he'd
Make *Adventures* into a libretto, though he couldn't say for whom.
By now Trewlany could. Berlioz for sure—crazy and theatrical as he
Had been himself. He tried to swim the river underneath Niagara falls—
What, compared with that, was Byron's sidestroke at the Hellespont?

Not much. And yet he struggled back to shore, defeated by the rapids.
And then returned to England. And then became a farmer there in
Monmouthshire to bide his time, waiting twenty years to write this
Memoir, tough as he could make it. He'd not admit *Adventures* had been
Fiction, but this was something else. This was Byron's ravaged legs
Underneath his shroud revealed as extreme deformity and source of all
His work. This was Shelley as a radical and atheist, not as an insipid
Angel made up by Victorians. This was Klephtes on Parnassus.

For it was they who had occupied the muses' home and fought
For Greece—Odysseus Androutses, leader of this tribe. He'd arisen on
The mountain as if he were the fictional De Reuter brought to life, giving
Tre his sister as a child-bride who then gave birth to Zella, phantom lost
In Java flame & spice & ambergris, but now reborn. And the mountain
Fastness was their ship, Ulysses' claim on history, Trelawny's last
Romantic stand. Byron stayed behind in Missolonghi to negotiate with
British agents, Philhellenic volunteers, Ulysses' enemy Mavrocordato.

IV

And there he died, bled to death by leeches meant to cure his fever.
When Odysseus was murdered, Trelawny held the cave. And even then
People went on walking out of books as he had out of *The Corsair*,
Hope's *Anastasius* coughing up young William Whitcomb. Here was an
Assassin drunk on Hope as he himself was drunk on Byron, both gone
Native with their turbans wrapped about them and their pistols
    bulging from
Their silken belts—fictions breaking into lethal fact, and broken.
Whitman shot Trelawny in the back. Parnassus merely shrugged.

And went on manifesting the sublime. In Usk, Trelawny wrote about
The elevation of a thousand feet above the plain, the rock face,
Projecting crags, the natural shelf of fractured stone, the great cave of
Galleries and chambers, vaulted roof. It was, he said, *like a cathedral*
When the softened light of evening or the moonlight made it glow. A place
Where traitor Anastasius might drive The Corsair back to doggerel.
Trelawny advertised the sale of his ewes & lambs, Herefords & mules,
Plows and other implements, wagons & an excellent light gig, his house.

He had designed two poets' boats, and now he quoted in his book the
Letter Shelley sent him praising the *Don Juan*, not however mentioning
That builders had reduced the size from thirty to just eighteen feet
Or that Byron's *Bolivar* would have an iron keel, copper fastenings,
Roomy cabin, deck, & ability to weather storms. *Don Juan* got a false
Stern & prow, was schooner rigged, required a ton of ballast . She was fast
But dangerous and *we must suppose*, wrote Shelley, *that the name was*
Given during sexual equivocation suffered by her godfather, Tre.

V

Was Shelley killed by sailors thinking that milord Inglese was on board
Don Juan with his pots of gold? Easy to confuse two boats, two
English poets, one of whom had written something even Leghorn
Fishermen might know, title of it on the stern. *A dying man had told his
Priest that his felucca with its seven men, its pointed bow and lateen
Sails had rammed the undecked boat off Via Reggio. It sank at once
In heavy weather and the sailors could not get aboard.* Thus Trelawny
To *The Times,* quoted without comment in his book . . .

Which he revises in his mind sitting for his portrait by Millais. He knows
Where he'll be buried, having dug the hole himself so long ago
In Rome. Right by Shelley. Right where he had gathered cedar cones
He'd planted on his farm . . . Maybe he should even be more graphic
Writing of the dead in Dervenakia, *the riders still astride the skeletons of
Horses and the bleached bones of negroes' hands still holding ropes
Attached to camels' skulls.* He'd seen three palikars impaled, still
Alive, the stakes that skewered them exiting their shoulders near the ear.

Millais has asked him please to hold the young girl's hand—a model
Brought to play the role of child or muse—she might have been the sister
Of Odysseus, might have been the phantom Zella—and he sees his
Fingers turn to bone—in the mirror on the wall his head become a skull
And that in turn the cup from which Lord Byron drank. He feels a dizziness
Turning into something else, into something that Millais can't paint,
Something no Victorian will take from him, no leaded type or print contain,
No word or image capture, no fire on beach or balustrade consume . . .

The Gondolier

I

. . .*Gehenna of the waters! Thou sea-Sodom!*
That's what Byron wrote and that's what Baron Corvo
Found eventually. After he was Pope. After he was back as Fr. Rolfe,
The "Fr." really Frederick, though he'd have you take it
Plainly for the "Father" he had failed to become. But he *had* become,
Through machinations of his own, *Hadrian VII*! Why not be top dog
Among the cats, whether in original Prooimion bed-sit or in
The pedophiliac back streets and rank canals of La Serenissima?

Whoever else had written his own life in earnest as the Holy Papa—
Chosen through the failure of Scrutiny and Compromise when
Providence itself made his pontificate the bull by which he'd
Horn his own dilemma with a gaggle of electors hanging on his tail?
Rolfe, Corvo, Rose: these and other singers hymned a heteronymic
Troubled soul—caviar, said D.H. Lawrence, spooned from the belly
Of a living fish. Autofisher from an obstinate isle, he'd flash & grasp
Obscenely as the others cast; *his* the One & True & Apostolic net.

Neologistic, too. He found the common dictionaries quite inadequate
And added supplemental volumes of his own. Dr. Johnson
Of the weird invention, odd etymology, unexpected spell: *Prooimion*
His *proheme, proheim, proem*: word becoming flesh and flesh
Becoming word, his world reduced to bed-sit Y-shaped room or
Coffin-cradle gondola in which he rowed—*oh might well have rowed*—
Tadzio to Aschenbach in 1911, the true Waladzio to Thomas Mann.
Proot proot he shouted at his patrons who were mules.

II

For mules they were, his patrons, and he'd give them what they
Merited in the invective of *Desire and Pursuit*. He'd write
His memoir as *roman à clef*, treble boys singing the castrati parts
In his *Venetian Vespers*. Cleft foot and cases of the clap
Would summon him once he hove in view: Clemency was not
His dwelling place among the clerisy, and Flavio, his cat,
Was better company than men. If the priest Da Ponte masqueraded
As a Casanova, Corvo might affect the pilgrim and the pimp.

Pilgrim not to *Hadrian's* Saint Peter's now. He sailed from his most
Eccentric book in topo, tacking in the Adriatic, musing on
The earthquake which was said to have been caused by the excess
Of eros in Venetian carnivals. His own vow of chastity had lasted
Twenty years, but only he himself and fiction's bishop-johnnies,
Owl-like hierarchs, had heard the call. His Vocation now in doubt, he
Sailed with his soul alone through winter seas, tsunami wave and
Blinding rain breaking on Calabria. Lights extinguished on the land.

In the morning of December 27, 1908, Crabbe discovers Zilda.
He searches for a cove by ruined villages and ties the topo to an oar
Driven in the sand. Hadrian VII now is Crabbe, Corvo is a sailor,
Zilda will be Zildo and then Zilda once again. Dead bodies,
Severed heads and limbs, lie all around. Zilda is descended from
A Doge: Falier Ermenegilda fu Bastian di Marin di Bastian di Marin
Is her name. She is a boy. He is a girl. Corvo doesn't know, but is
Frederick William Serafino Austin Louis Mary Rolfe...

III

And pulls her from the wreckage of La Tasca, pulls him by
His heels from the pork-chop-bones, the wood-ash & the rags.
She has no breasts, but neither has he parts. A penis would resolve
An ambiguity even in the presence of a Dodge. She'll be his
Servant; he'll earn his keep as second gondolier. Crabbe doesn't
Watch her change his sodden clothes and put on light. But then he
Stares: a creature in his world who isn't of this world, *a boy
By intention but a girl. Nature has been interrupted in her work.*

He writes it in his book. A book he thinks will either save
Or damn his soul. He comes about, sails back to Venice with his
Miracle. Zildo watches quietly. This aging man can struggle
With the boat all day and write all through the night. And what does
He write about? They agree that Z will be a boy for the eyes
Of Venetians and the English Colony and the Reale Societa
Canottieri Bucintoro. He writes *I beg to apply for a situation as
A Gondolier.* He writes *The Desire and Pursuit of the Whole.*

Z warns Crabbe of winter storms, the wake of passing
Steam boats that can swamp the pupparin in which they'll sleep
Now the topo's sold. They ply the waters, unlicensed boatmen.
They swim together in the great Lagoon. Crabbe writes his tirades
Cribbing Corvo's letters to the men who helped him after
The assassination of the Pope he had become. His friends would
Kill him once again, encourage him to starve, watch him freezing
In a gondola tied up at nights to a crumbling palace wall.

IV

He denounces Benson to the bishop, names him Bonson
In his book; he denounces Pirie-Gordon ("Caliban") to publishers,
Taylor to Society of Law. *I have not slept or changed my clothes
In fifteen nights. In the fortnight I've had four lunches, two dinners,
Three breakfasts, teas at the Bucintoro club where I gobble all the
Crusts the members leave behind. Toad-eater and most cretinous
Of men, I offer you the sixty rats I've trapped since Monday last.
I offer you my bitterest execrations, former friend.*

He promises to write pornography and publish it in Pirie-Gordon's
Name. He'll put his patron's arms on the cover by authority
Of Sanctissima Sophia. Z finds him boys among the tyro gondoliers
And Corvo offers them to well-connected men in London who
Will pay him for a connoisseur's advice. He describes in letters lewd
And rare lascivious acts, the special skills of Z's young friends,
But doesn't put this in his book. *Sea-Sodom, Sea-Sodom*: Rocking in
His boat and writing with his large fountain pen in colored inks.

He's acquired his rules of punctuation reading Addisson. Punctual
As always, he meets the German for a journey to the Lido.
The German is a maestro celebrated by the world. He himself is
No-man, No-man, but Z is holy light. *Deus in adjutorium
Meum intende . . . me festina . . .* Monteverdi's Vespers, 1610,
Echoes from St Mark's. *Dixit Dominus . . . until I make thine
Enemies thy footstool.* No, he has no license but he knows from
Z what Herr Professor Meistersinger doesn't know he wants.

V

Corvo wants the recognition he deserves, wants his books
In print, wants his former friends to pony up their patronage,
Wants what Crabbe desires—*Tou holou oun tei epitumiai
Dioxei eros onoma*—To be whole in love. The old Duchess
Sforza-Cesarini might have loved him once, gave at any rate
A title to him and a small estate. And his "special friends"?
All turned against him. All to be assassinated in his book.
Who'd suppose from *Hadrian* he'd seize on the *Symposium*?

Crabbe staggers in the cemetery on the isle of Sanmichele.
He brings his gifts. This is where they bury strangers like himself.
White chrysanthemums and rose buds for an English engineer,
A baby in the columbarium. It's the Day of the Dead in Venice;
Earth a flooded ossuary now. He goes back to his boat, lies down
On his back while chanting *Kyrie eleèson* to himself, the waters
Rocking in response: . . . Then the black light, then . . . *che ragion
Tu ne hai aver 'l amante e no verdelo mai* . . . Zildo singing, Zilda's

Blood dripping from her arm: *Scusie, Sior, but I found you dead
And fed you ikor and you live*—lives like another who will die
Inside himself until he steps upon uneven paving stones in Paris
And the Venice of his youth floods into him like
Combray had done when he sucked from the *madeleine* mere tea
As if it were the blood of all his past—*you live!*
Though Corvo died, seeking to be Zildo's catechumen,
No mere Pope, no Hadrian, no liege of Sforza-Cesarini or
   Guermantes.

[69]

The Housekeeper

I

      Lac Léman, he'd said. And told her that was where
Lord Byron and Madam de Staël had stayed, where
He had first got something right about unconscious memory. He'd
Ended one book there in order to begin the great unfinished one
That she was part of, that everyone he'd known was part of,
That would in the end restore the works of time in place
Of places that at first appeared to wash them all beyond recall like
Ripples from a boat across Geneva's lake . . .

At least that's what she thought he'd said. This man Belmont
Again had asked her to explain what she'd explained
Already. It was, she saw, a kind of test. He'd ask the same question
Several times and watch her closely. Once again she'd answer
As she had before. *Lac Léman*, she said he'd said. *And suddenly
Sensation of congruence & a joy altogether inexplicable until the ripples
From a boat converge from memory's Beg-Meil* & she says *Time it's
Time for you to go* and he says *Sodomite certainly Monsieur*

As everyone but you maintains and she says *No I would have known
Since I knew everything and anyway you've asked me this
A dozen times.* She has her tests for him as well. Who is he, after all?
A friend of Henry Miller, the American pornographer. Monsieur
Has now been dead for sixty years. Do the young read Henry Miller in
Translations by Belmont? He uses words Monsieur would never
Want to see in print. Nor would she, a woman over eighty—but not
Without desire. For the truth at least, spoken into a machine.

II

That whirs like Krapp's last tape. Georges Belmont has told her
About Beckett and his play in which an old man speaks into a little
Microphone reciting memories of his past like she does now—Beckett
Yet another one of Belmont's friends who wrote about Monsieur.
He reads to her from *Sodom and Gomorrah* where she's called by her
Own name, a maid in Balbec at the Grand Hotel. She speaks there as
*She did of Monsieur as a bird, pecking his croissant and preening
Feathers, deep-eyed mischief, raven hair.* Has she read the passage?

Has she read the book? Did she say that to him, Belmont asks, or did
He make it up? *How much of his book have you been reading in these
Sixty years?* Another test. She wonders if he'll put words in her
Mouth. She's heard he had another name, was in the Occupation busy
In suspicious ways. It's one thing to be friends with Henry Miller and
Another with the Vichy bureaucrats working with Pétain, Pierre Laval.
Belmont carries on about the Sodomites. He'll be, she understands, her
Voice and vehicle, the presence of her past in some dim future.

She says *he'd have his coffee just exactly so. Night turned to day
And day to night. Everything was upside down. Time did not have hours,
Only things to do.* Like him she was a bird but one that sang and
Hopped from branch to branch. She brought the water bottles made
The fire delivered letters for him cleaned the room if he were out and
Picked up all the towels he dropped. *He awoke at four p.m. and wrote
All night, eating almost nothing. He shut out all the sun and burned
The powders that would help him breathe. He disconnected phones.*

III

Her own phone rings. She picks it up. *No, she says, I'm far too busy
And I will be for some time.* But she chats politely for a moment
While Belmont thumbs a copy of *Le Monde* with articles on Watergate,
Although he's thinking about Dreyfus and not Nixon. He's thinking
About loyalty and then he thinks about the very awkward case of
Georges Pelerson. He *is* Georges Pelerson. Celeste hangs up and then
Begins at once where she left off: *Yes, yes the cork lined walls the sealed
Windows fires in summer winter coats. Yes, yes he'd been a Dreyfusard.*

*You know all that. He wouldn't flee the city in the war. He had a special
Kind of courage. I'd go to the basement; he'd go out into the night.* He
Asks her if she still remembers doing Gide, her parody of *Les Nourritures*,
And she says *Oh Nathanaël, I will speak to thee of Monsieur's lady friends.
There is she who made him go out after many years, taxi to the Ritz,
Bell-hops, tips, exhaustion.* And of course Monsieur did go out to the Ritz,
Though not with Gide. Belmont's working nights on *Fear of Flying*;
Suddenly he's got the French for that repeating phrase, *a zippered fuck* . . .

History's a tangle here, but he will sort it all out in the book. *No, she says,
He never lived in Le Cuziat's male brothel; yes I'm sure Agostinelli
Wasn't Albertine. It's true he went out in the night to watch a flagellation
As research. And other ghastly acts. He'd tell me all about them just
As if he'd been to some soirée at Countess Greffulhe's. All analysis and
Distance, objectivity. No he didn't drink much alcohol or take those
Drugs you say but just caffeine & powders though he disinfected letters and
Could only look through windows at the hawthorn he had loved.*

IV

Of course she was a prisoner, she knows that. Everyone he knew
Became a prisoner of his book, but there they'll live in time
Beyond their times. Belmont still fears he'll live as Pelerson, who
Swept away his footprints leading to her door. In 1982 Maria Jolas
Will declare that Georges Belmont does not exist, that she and
Joyce and Beckett only knew a Georges Pelerson, collaborationist, who
Calls himself another name & hasn't a remembrance of things past.
In 1982 *Monsieur Proust* will be a German movie called *Céleste*—

Music by Quartet Bartholdy playing César Franck. *No, she says, it's
Altogether nonsense that Monsieur set out for that quartet to
Play the Franck carrying a large tureen of soup. He did awake them, one
By one, and brought them back at great expense to play for him. He
Needed one more time to hear the little phrase and all its metamorphoses.*
(Belmont's now forgotten his solution for *a zippered fuck*.) *Monsieur
Once found himself at dinner next to Churchill's table at the time of
Peace talks at Versailles. Then I nearly died of Spanish influenza.*

But the quartet. He asks once more if that was 1916 and, if there was no
Tureen of soup, didn't she provide some fried potatoes and champagne
When they arrived? She says *he wept the day Jaurés was shot; he hated
War but loved his country. Franck and France. They played for him the same
Year as Verdun.* She doesn't ask *Were you a Nazi?* and he rewinds just
A bit and thinks of Krapp in Beckett saying *spool spoooool—box three &
Spool five* and then of Nixon quoted in *Le Monde* maintaining *No erasures
On those tapes.* She thinks about the index in that book he has, her name.

V

*P spends time in conversation with; burns P's notebooks; taking P's
Dictation; pasting manuscripts; parody of Gide; finding spectacles for P . . .*
It's like a tape, a movie. Click & whir and flipping over pages in the
Third biography: *Burns his notebooks & There aren't any gaps!* Krapp is
Saying *Face she had! The eyes!* Georges Belmont is saying *Pelerson*
At some tribunal, disappearing for a decade without civil rights but with
The Henry Millers, *Capricorn* for starters, and a new career that's
Brought him, very busy, to her side. He told her *You must trust me!*

She feels like a theme in César Franck's sonata or a train ride to Cabourg—
A transcribed interview, a Google search before its time. For years they've
Sought her out and she has kept her silence. Alone all night he practiced
Death but also resurrection in the word, *déflagration*. Results 1–10
Of some 1,000 for *Céleste Albaret* (0.11 seconds): Poster, News, & Forum,
See new play at Steppenwolf . . . *an unlettered girl lived a dream. She was
The confidante & maid & mother surrogate. . .* Or was that *Poster-nude,
A fettered girl*? She doesn't say *And you, were you the Jugendfüher?*

She says again *It's time for you to go.* He will not find the sky outside all
Full of Gothas, Zeppelins, or the biwing Valkyries spiraling in spotlit
Crossbeams up. He's coming down from what for seven weeks has kept
Him high. She doesn't say *I loved him* and he doesn't ask *Did he love you?*
She says *Monsieur liked the Abbé Mugnier who used to say Of course
We know that Hell exists, but no one's in it.* She asks *And all these people
Reading Henry Miller or Miss Jong—why not read Monsieur instead?*
He says, *They don't have time.* She smiles . . . And then he's gone . . . .

Through her window spring pollens blow & settle over miles & miles.

Epilogue: Four Seasons of Vladimir Dukelsky

I—Winter

              . . . and the Winter Palace stormed.
Place where khaki tall Kerensky
Felt the fire Scriabin fanned at everything provisional in his *Prometheus*.
He'd huff and puff and blow down what was hardly built.
Crew-cut Angel Gabriel with sex appeal, Dukelsky said of K.
Dukelsky—hot Kiev Conservatory music-man whose own angelic
Sex appeal took the form of Debussy pastiche,
Aladdine & Palomide his *Pelléas*.

Would K play Melisande all dressed in skirt and head scarf
Fleeing commissars who paid Dukelsky in potatoes, rice and peas
For a revolutionary hymn *à la* Glazunov? Newly beggared
Vladimir, obliged to drink a tea he made from bark & carrots,
Wore an avant-garde green coat his mother cut from
Billiard-table baize, shirt and trousers that
Had been the winter curtains in his late father's room. He thought he heard
A turbine buzzing somewhere in augmented fourths.

Modus diaboli! Cheka spies all whispering in Tristan's
Tritones and diminished fifths. He missed the Maeterlinck Express
From Kiev to Odessa, clicking down the rails chromatically
From C-sharp on to G to conjure fields full of fauns with double flutes.
He took the typhus train, hand & handkerchief to mouth & nose
For more than fifteen days of unrelenting plague.
He hummed the *Marseillaise*: *En-fants*: a fourth. *Pa-trie*, a fourth again.
His mother, *ancien régime*, hid two diamonds up her snatch.

II—Spring

And they escaped. What month was it, Paris? What week in New York?
In Constantinople you could hardly tell. In Odessa they had fled
The rearing horses at the gate, the Red Cavalry, the panic, mobs.
Navaho had pushed through ice behind *St. Andrew*, snow and fog
Obscuring Bosphorus for the listing Motherland's ancient ship of refugees.
Yok, Yok, Effendi sang the foxtrotting girls; and Tommies drunk on
Turkish beer demanded *Tipperary, K-K-K-Katy*, from the salon trio
At Tokatlian's café. Dukelsky played for silent films most anything he chose.

It was a job. Glazunov for Westerns, Mussorgsky's "Pictures"
For the Chaplins and some Rimsky-Korsakov for Lang's *Metropolis*.
One night at the Tokatlian he heard a thing he liked. They called it *Swanee*.
The boys in the native band with gusle, oud, and zourna
Made it sound like someone's jihad on the boil, but he heard the
Gershwin somehow coming through. *Yok, Yok, Effendi, it is not beloved
By the authorities but Yanks and Limeys ask for it and "Hindustan."*
He memorized it on the spot; it finally felt like spring.

When he reached New York he played the gypsy schmaltz required
For the eateries like Samovar on Second Avenue. He scored
A hooker's favorite songs for fifty cents a piece. His secret life was
Briefly all dodecaphonic when he met the man whose *Swanee* he
Had whistled on the decks of *King Alexander* on his way to an
Ellis Island transit. *Don't fear lowbrow, Kid*, he said; *Tin Pan Alley
Is okay. If you haven't got a melody you ain't American. Heat me up
Some ragtime. We'll change that longhair name to Vernon Duke.*

III—Summer

But he was not yet American, even after he prepared his friend's
Rhapsody in Blue for two pianos. His mother sold her diamonds to
An underworld dealer and sent him off to Paris where Diaghilev
Disparaged Duke for vaudeville gigs & rags but commissioned something
Neoclassical and Russian from Dukelsky: *Tutus with Kokoshniks,*
As he said. Enter Flora, lifted high by Zephyrus, dancing *pas de deux*
In an Anacreontic light. The waltz, mazurka, variations & *divertissements
Des muses*: They would even make a corpse dance, said Prokofiev.

Dukelsky still was only twenty-two. The critics liked him. Poulenc
And Stravinsky were impressed, and he got a check for 6,000 francs
And an invitation from Diaghilev to come along to London with the show.
Cocteau, however, slapped him with a glove: *Les Parisiens t'envoyent
De la merde!* But when pressed in earnest for a choice between the swords
And pistols, he sang out: *Embrassons-nous!* Degas had said to Whistler
That he dressed as if he had no talent, Gershwin wrote to D. And D to G:
I wish my talent didn't sometimes wear a pretty little frilly frock.

He felt a little less Dukelsky, started feeling Duke. Economies would soon
Be on the rocks, Zephyrus and Flora on the dole. Would there be a
Space to occupy between an Ogden Nash and Mandelstam? He'd set them
Both to music in the end. Certain words he'd dare to write himself:
*Glittering crowds & shimmering clouds in canyons of steel. Jaded roués
And gay divorcées who lunch at the Ritz.* He thought about the autumn
In New York. Why did it seem so inviting? It was 1928 and he took
Another ship. Like Mandelstam in *Epitaph*, he wrapped a rose in furs.

IV—Autumn

Diaghilev soon died, and Gershwin shortly after. Dukelsky grasped at
Balanchine, the movies. Émigré composers headed for L.A. as
Wall Street crashed and Sunset Boulevard survived. Prokofiev heckled him
From Moscow about *maids who become prostitutes to feed their mums*.
His mother ate. He wrote his songs: *April in Paris* on a tuneless upright
In the back of West Side Tony's bistro; *Words Without Music* for
The Ziegfield Follies, 1936. Duke would dig Dukelsky from the rubble
Of Depression. Dancers kicked their can-cans on the silver screen.

But did Dukelsky dig the tunes of Duke? Count Basie would in time,
Sinatra would—and, born on his own birthday, even Thelonius Monk.
Can you play again, Sam Goldwyn asked him laughing, *that dyspeptic chord*?
Musicologists have praised the two adjacencies preceding an initial E,
The lower raised chromatically to match the half step in a symmetry:
A-pril in Par-is. Meanwhile, Mandelstam still lived, weeping for
The wooden Russia of his youth. *Gradually the servants sort out piles
Of overcoats. They wrap a rose in furs*. In Cyrillic and for choir, an epitaph.

For whom? Diaghilev? Dukelsky? Mandelstam? Academic serialism
Shut down tonal elegists and Tin Pan Alley crooners came to terms
With Elvis after yet another World War. Who remembered the bucolic
Zephyrus, phantasmagoric *Epitaph* for choir? Alexander Feodorovich
Kerensky hummed a phrase stuck in his head from something that he
   couldn't
Name and walked the Stanford campus in the twilight to his little office
Where he wrote a book about the Revolution no one read. He wrapped
A rose in furs & it was autumn: in Leningrad & Paris, Palo Alto & New York.

III
The Cotranslator's Dilemmas

In Memory of Göran Printz-Påhlson

The Cotranslator's Dilemma

Again the e-mail draft appears on my screen.
I go back to work.
Tranströmer's successor speaks aloud from his poem.
Sort of, that is. I'm supposed to make such improvements
that everyone in America will recognize at a flash
the original style & voice, the very personality of this poet
known up to now only by his most intimate friends.
I despair. They are waiting in Lund for my version.
But it's already in English, so what should I do?
I change an article: "*The* cow in the pasture" would really
be better written here "*A* cow in the pasture."
I stare at the screen. Maybe a comma just before the conjunction.
At just that moment I hear a commotion in the hall.
I can hear several people questioning students:
Which is the charlatan's office? I recognize the Swedish accents.
Suddenly Jesper and Leif, Göran and Lars-Håkan
all tumble into my room. We're here to help you, they laugh.
Göran offers me a virtual beer.
The heart of your problem, Leif says in Swedish,
Is that you don't know Swedish. What?
He says in English: The problem is you don't know Swedish.
Oh, that. Well, I work from this other guy's drafts.
What do you do? He seems to have a whole list of questions.
I show him the screen: "*A* cow" was once "*The* cow", I say,
and commas, or their absence, are very important.
That's it? he asks. Nothing else?
Well, there's the issue of prepositions. I find that most
Of my Swedish colleagues get confused:
A poet whose head is up in the clouds may appear with
his head up *around* the clouds, or up *about* the clouds,
or even up *from* or up *off* the clouds!
The four Swedes sputter with amusement or contempt.
So that's all? Articles, prepositions and commas?
Well, sometimes, if I'm lucky.

And what if you're not? Not lucky, that is.
Ah, then—I hesitate—then I have to rewrite the poem.
You'd re-write somebody's poem?
Not in Swedish, of course, I hasten to say. Just in English.
Ah well, they grumble, that's a relief.
I mean, what can you do with a poem set entirely in Lapland
that's full of *yoiks* or *voulles*? And then he throws in
classical myths and quotes not only from Sappho but also Rimbaud.
American readers will never sort it all out.
American readers could learn to yoik for themselves, Jesper insists.
In this poem with a cow? I mean, I say,
in the poem that appeared on my screen containing *the* cow.
The one whose poet had his head up around the clouds.
Apollo and Hermes are also, I can see, there on the screen,
and what am I to do with words like *Poikilóthronos* and *Boukólos*?
Well, Lars-Håkan says, what *will* you do?
I'll change the setting entirely, move the lot of them to Texas!
But in Texas nobody yoiks, everyone protests.
There are plenty of cows, however, and cowboys like to yell & shout
while they ride all around saying things like *Yahoo*!
But a Yoik is a Lapland poem, it's a chant, an incantation, a song!
In my Texas version the cowboys will sing quite a lot:
Get along little dogie, and stuff like that.
That's the line in fact that I'll substitute for the quote from Rimbaud.
What about Hermes? What about Apollo?
I think I'll exchange them for John Wayne & Clint Eastwood.
Those are mythic types American readers relate to.
All the Swedes have now stopped grinning & laughing
and are starting to cry, tearing their hair.
In Greek plays lots of people cry and tear their hair.
That's another thing that gets into this poem, along with the
language itself: the *Poikilóthronoses* and *Boukóloses*.
Sounds like some bacteria infecting the meat of the burger.
Göran says, darting a knowing glance over at Jesper:

The author of this poem is an eminent Hellenist!
By God, I thought he was a Swede!
Anyway, if you've got to have your Greek go see Ezra Pound.
He's long dead, of course, which means
you might as well just go on working with me.
I've become a little tipsy by this point drinking the virtual beer
and suddenly drop the nearly empty virtual bottle onto the keyboard.
Yoiks! We're all at once transported off to Amazon.com
The Amazon: Now that's better than Texas!
The stern-wheeler is sailing upriver from Santarém.
Elizabeth Bishop is getting on board, clutching
an empty wasp's nest given to her by the druggist
in the town's little blue pharmacy. I follow her with my cow
which has somehow attracted a herd—
not of cattle exactly, but of sheep, goats, yaks,
chickens, llamas, cats and yellow dogs.
What's going on? I'm not exactly sure, but I like it.
Jesper's shouting in English: Who do you think you are,
some kind of Hercules? That poem (that golden girdle!) is mine;
I, I, I, am Tranströmer's successor!
Not any more, I exclaim, heading into the current
on the riverboat called *Poikilóthronos Juan*.
Off in wintry Lund, all the systems start to crash.
Every screen flickers and goes blank.

Jesper Svenbro: Five Poems

Idiolect

In my use of the word "world" there is a strangeness
which I have never been able to shake:
the word carries a hopefulness
which has no strict foundation
in the real world.
The world being what it is!
For although I know it cannot be used
in the sense I want to give it
it is the same picture that faithfully
returns in my memory
whenever I pronounce it to myself—
it is the light space over my childhood,
white April sun over a province
whose horizon trembles in the distance:
The world rests over there.
It is the late 1940s. In those days
I went to Sunday school every week
in our northern Galilee. To me
Palestine was still a country
with heights, fields, and rivers such as ours;
and by a miracle
the hills of Rönneberga just outside of town
became the light green mountain
where on one spring day Jesus
had said to his pupils: "Go out into the whole world!"
Languages were buzzing in the air.
Jews, Arabs, Kappadocians, Egyptians!
We were in the Holy Land,
coltsfoots were blooming
along the ditch-banks of the whole world.
And among all the tongues that I heard
was also the sound of my own

Translated with Lars-Håkan Svensson

Out There

Ever since I started writing poems
(and maybe even further back than that)
the words "out there" have seemed to carry distant messages:
As if a strange power emanated from them
when I say them over slowly deep inside
or write them down, lending equal emphasis
to both as two short words.
Over the years I have slowly understood
where this charge is coming from, from what landscape
they derive their supernatural light.
In memory I return to my native city,
Sturegatan 1, 4th floor, the window to the yard
with a view of a little pond in the north northeast:
about three miles away you could just see Härslöv
nearly a hundred yards above the sea
while in the elongated heights to the east
the hills of Ronneberga rose
beyond my vision. This was the view
from the nursery I shared with my sisters,
from the world I knew so well
with its doll's house and my hobby horse
on green rockers . . . I saw out there
on many late afternoons in my childhood
the landscape bathing in sunlight.
And I imagined that two cyclists had stopped out there;
and if I could see them so clearly, it must mean
that they were supernatural in size
where they stood gazing in the direction of the Sound
which was beyond the range of vision too.
They are my parents who have just gotten off their bikes,
my father in a shirt with rolled up sleeves:
looking at the glitter of the sea with screwed-up eyes,

my mother with closed eyes, in a summer dress:
the mild summer light falls on their faces,
so beautiful that in that moment
they must have been touched by the divine—
while the breeze fills my father's loose white shirt
and slowly blows through the locks
of my mother's hair, who is still closing her eyes
in the light of the late afternoon.

                    Translated with Lars-Håkan Svensson

Ionian

The light in the north Sound was "Ionian"—
greedily we repeated the word although we didn't know
what sense to make of it at all—
until one day we cycled seaward on our bikes
from well inland and at last high upon a hill beheld
the summer water resting there against the light,
glittering intangibly as far as we could see
as if a massive door had opened on infinity.
Ionian was the tone throbbing in the sky,
Ionian the dialect of waves, Ionian as well
the dry white sands along the beach. We had found
the tone that seemed to hold reality together,
like a hub that sings around its axis
with a note of an "Ionian" frequency—
while Ionian white clouds scudded quickly on the wind
in formation spreading out across the sky.
On days like that you would see the pillars of Heracles
shimmering unreal in the distance like mirages
where the Sound is narrowest: the streams
were swift and deep up there, the water
cold and flowing from the depths
into the inland sea, into its warm and amber summer.
The clouds: an Ionian archipelago in the north.
It was as if our very thought had ionized—
the most trivial ideas now were charged electrically
and seemed to wander slowly, white to blue.
Everything was colored by the adjective and it was spoken
ever and forever over whining voids, increasingly monotonous,
so often used that finally it
became unusable. Invisible in white. As if the door
was closed and painted over, sealing

our Ionian epoch. And after many years I passed it
and was able without strain to lift it off—
I took down the lintel, the door-posts and threshold:
all that remained was the key-hole
now that the light of my late summer afternoon
had neither attributes nor hinges. No keys, no handle.
All the paint had flaked off and was gone.
The evening sea was wide and blue. Its warmth
a feeling over my entire face.

                    Translated with Lars-Håkan Svensson

Pont Mirabeau, c 1895

The lady on the Pont Mirabeau raising her arm
to salute us, waving in a painting by Henri Rousseau,
seemed to me unsurpassed in melancholy:
the afternoon sky a golden ground
beyond the bridge master's house to the left,
beyond the bridge
and beyond the trees of the park
on the other side of the river waves.
The tricolor has just been hoisted on the boat
on this side of the bridge.
As I now recall the painting,
the colors are summer bright, almost "joyful,"
Therefore, the silhouette of the shadowy dark lady
becomes increasingly blacker—
as if epitomizing
absence itself against the sky.
The entire pain of leave-taking is in her gesture.
How deeply loss has been anticipated here!
But since we see her against the light
it is impossible to say if she is turning her back to us
or if she's turning towards us:
if she's looking off to the southwest
sunlight is falling on her face
(which we are never going to see);
if she is turned towards us, it is in the shadow
(and we can only imagine her features).
In other words, we do not know
if her gaze is turned in the same direction as ours
and she is raising her hand to greet
someone who is disappearing down the river
or if it is we who are now disappearing upstream
and receive her greeting.
We see her for the last time.

But conversely it is equally possible
that it is we who are approaching her while
traveling downstream.
As if we have been apart for years
and are at long last returning
(How pleased she is to see us again!)
Finally it is of course also possible
that we are witnessing someone else's return
—the way she sees it, from a point far behind her—
and that the old world here is being
shipped back upstream, and I
suddenly find that I am waving,
waving like her, waving
to someone whom I once loved, to the days
which are now gloriously returning upstream in the late sun,
maybe by a barge, whose tricolor has been hoisted:
everything has been exempted from duty
in this golden hour.
But I will never ever see
the features of her face as she waves from her bridge,
waves, waves incessantly,
I will never ever know
if this is a farewell
or a return,
nor whose farewell or return
the painting is about.
For a moment the picture seems to beam
with all its possibilities:
it becomes at once a homecoming and a farewell.
And the woman is brightly shining darkness.
It is an afternoon
almost a century ago.
The sky a golden ground beyond the bridge.

       Translated with Lars-Håkan Svensson

Stalin as Wolf

The position of the wolf was once secure in political theory
before it was driven by urbanization back to that final wilderness,
e.g. Siberia, where it lingers still without, to anyone's notice,
affecting contemporary politics. The plains sparkle in sunlight
as a helicopter rushes over the landscape: stunted birches
appear and disappear out on the snow covered tundra
where all at once a wolf can be seen: it runs, it trips,
looks backward: someone has edited-in the hot gasps
of a dog to make us hear its fear: it is filmed close-up
and the camera is slightly jarred when the helicopter gunner
fires. The wolf is hit, rolls over in a swirl of snow,
then everything is still. Every year in the Soviet Union
more than 22,000 wolves were killed according to recent
statistics, and perhaps it is even yet a silent requirement
of Russian polity—menacing, inaccessible—which would explain
the cynical, obsessive precision of the hunting methods
both in the filmed sequence noted above, which,
with no comment, introduced a documentary on modern Siberia,
and also on the inner tundra where the wolf howls with hunger
in a nightmare only partially reclaimable. The facts about wolves
in Sweden at my disposal allow no conclusions, and yet,
within its territory, the wolf has developed local, independent
clans which have been identified as distinctive species. About
the role of the wolf in Russian politics 1875–1953, however,
we know more than we suppose: Stalin's most wolf-like characteristic
was distrust, which grew in proportions never foreseen by classical
lupine theory. As early as in Aesop we can find sufficient examples
to maintain that Stalin's role in political theory is basic:
the Wolf as Butcher, masters to perfection the partition technique
which is the base of political equality. The jaws of the wolf
equal the Knife, and classical myth provides again the scenario

which ought to have haunted us earlier: hunting the Wolf became
in the Thirties a dominant trait in Soviet politics; he who wrote
"All power to the Soviets" three years before Kronstadt was now
the uncontested Butcher, the principle of absolute mistrust
had triumphed over Equality and the pack closed ranks around Stalin
in the whirling snowstorm. The Bolsheviks had certainly planned
an equitous banquet of wolves, but forgotten the moment when Knife
turns into Weapon and the feast into its opposite. The gasps
haunt me, the plains sparkle, the film invades the memory:
am I willing to test that project now when Stalin's crimes
are rostered and surveyed, now when his blood-thirst, along with
the prospects which made it possible, have all been analysed?
Zoologists can emend, on essential points, classical mythology,
refract the Stalinoid language: lacking both project and theory
the pack makes real the apothegm: "To each according to his need,
from each according to his ability." It refutes the picture
that pursues me and, in the end, obliges me to abandon
my language: gazing at Stalin, letting the wolf run off.

Translated with Göran Printz-Påhlson

Göran Printz-Påhlson: Two Poems

Sir Charles Babbage Returns to Trinity College *After Having Commissioned the Swedish Mechanic Scheutz to Build a Difference Engine. On the Bank of the River Cam He Gazes at the Bridge of Sighs and Contemplates the Life of the Dragonfly*

No man can add an inch to his height, says the Bible. Yet once I saw the detective Vidocq change his height by circa an inch and a half. It has always been my experience that one ought to maintain the greatest accuracy even in the smallest things.

    No one has taught me more than my machine. I know that a law of nature is a miracle. When I see the dragonfly, I see its nymph contained in its glittering flight. How much more probable it is that any one law will prove to be invalid than it will prove to be sound. It must happen in the end: although the wheels and levers all move accurately enough, the *other* number will appear, the unexpected, the incalculable, when the nymph bursts into a dragonfly. I see a hand in life, the unchanging hand of The Great Effacer.

    Therefore be scrupulous and guard your reason, in order that you may recognize the miracle when it occurs. I wrote to Tennyson that his information was incorrect when he sang "every minute dies a man, / Every minute one is born." In fact, every minute one and one-sixteenth of a man is born. I refuse to abandon this one-sixteenth of a man.

Translated with the author

Man-Made Monster Surreptitiously Regarding Idyllic Scene *in Swiss Hermitage, a Copy of Goethe's "Werther" Resting in its Lap*

It is sometimes considered to be an advantage to start from scratch. I myself would be the first to admit that my maker did a good job when he constructed my brain, although it must be said that he was unsuccessful with my outer appearance: my ongoing programme of self-education has provided me with many a happy hour of intellectual satisfaction. Spying on these touching family tableaux unobserved makes me nevertheless both excited and dejected. I suspect that only with the greatest of difficulties shall I myself be able to establish meaningful relationships with other beings. It is not so much my disfigured countenance which distresses me—I have accustomed myself to that by gazing at it in a nearby tarn and now find it, if not immediately attractive, then, at least, captivating: in particular the big screws just under my ears which my maker insisted on putting there for God knows what purpose, accentuate my expression of virile gravity and ennui—as rather a certain lack of elegance and animal charm. It seems for instance to be almost impossible for me to find a suit that fits as it should. One of my more casual acquaintances, a certain Count Dracula, whom I vaguely remember having encountered in some circumstances or other—regrettably I cannot remember where or when—is in this respect much more fortunate: I envy him his relaxed manner of deporting himself in evening dress, but I have to admit that I cannot understand the reason for his negative (and extremely selfish) attitude to his environment. For myself, it seems as if my background and construction limit the possibilities for the successful development of my personality in socially acceptable forms. Evidently, I must choose between two possible careers: either to seek self-expression in the pursuit of crime—within which vast and varied field of activity sexual murder ought to offer unsurpassed opportunities for a creature of my disposition—or during my remaining years quietly to warm my hands at the not altogether fantastically blazing but nonetheless never entirely extinguished fires of scholarship.

Translated with the author

Tomas Tranströmer

Baltic Seas III

In a dim corner of the Gotland church, color of mild mold
there is a christening font of sandstone—12th century—the stonemason's
    name
still there, glowing
like a row of teeth in a mass grave:
                    HEGWALDR
                            the name remains.

  And his pictures
here and on the sides of other crocks, swarms of people, shapes emerging
    from the stone.
The nuclei of goodness and evil in their eyes are bursting there.
Herod at the table: the cock in the serving dish flies up and crows
    Christus natus est—the waiter was executed—
close by the child is born, under clusters of faces dignified and helpless
    like young monkeys.
And the fleeing footfalls of the pious
echoing across the gaping dragonscaled sewers
(The images stronger in memory than when directly observed, stronger
when the font turns in the slow rumbling roundabout of memory.)
Nowhere shelter. Everywhere risk.
As it was. As it is.
Only inside is there peace, in the water of the font which nobody sees,
but on the outer sides the struggle goes on.
And peace may come drip by drip, perhaps at night
when we are unaware,
or as when one is on drips in a hospital ward.

Men, beasts, ornaments.
There is no landscape. Ornaments.

Mr. B*** my fellow-tourist, amiable, exiled,
realeased from Robben Island, says:
"I envy you. I feel nothing for nature.
But *people in a landscape*, that tells me something."

Here are people in a landscape.
A photograph from 1865. A steam-launch anchored at the quay in the
    inlet.
Five figures. A lady in light crinoline, like a bell, like a flower.
The men look like extras in a rustic play.
All of them are handsome, hesitating on the verge of fading out,
They disembark for a while. They fade out entirely.
The steam-launch is an obsolete model—
high funnel, sun tent, narrow hull—
it is utterly alien, a UFO which has landed.
Everything else in the photograph is shockingly real:
the ripples on the water,
the other shore—
I can rub my hand across the rugged rocks,
I can hear the whispering of the wind in the spruce trees.
It is near. It is
today.
The waves are contemporary.

Now, a hundred years later. The waves come from *no man's water*
and pound against the rocks.
I walk along the shore. It isn't as it used to be to walk along the shore.
One has to yearn for so much, speak to many people at once, live with
    such thin walls.
Every object has got a new shadow behind the ordinary shadow
and you hear it dragging along even when it is entirely dark.

It is night.

The strategic planetarium turns. The lenses stare into darkness.
The nocturnal sky is full of numbers, and they are being fed
Into a flashing box,
a piece of furniture
which contains the energy of a swarm of locusts eating acres of crops of Somalia in half an hour.

I don't know if we are at the beginning or at the terminal stage.

Recapitulation cannot be made, recapitulation is impossible.

Recapitulation is the mandrake root—
(*vide* the Dictionary of Superstitions:
                          MANDRAKE
                                    magical herb
which let out such a terrfying scream when it was pulled out of the ground
that one would fall down dead. The dog had to do it . . .)

                    Translated with Göran Printz-Påhlson

Göran Sonnevi

From **Mozart Variations**
(Surviving lines of an unfinished translation made
with Göran Printz-Påhlson, 1984–1986)

∼

Mozart and the whiteness of morning

∼

a face which has cut off, white

as a physical pain
close to the unendurable—

∼

Inscrutable humankind, violent

listen to the sounds
the silence grows inside me, a huge cone
a funnel
sucking me up into space

so it was
when I had the entire world
growing in my belly, the globe
just grew and grew, and I rose and rose
a tiny shape
on the infinite surface
shouted, cried
from there, to you, out of my mouth
came letter-sculpted blocks
of silence

~

Flowering hawthorn

The smell of grass
and under the green,
the shell of a small snail

and breaks up my face

series on series of abstract transformations

~

The first shapes of an infinite fear break
out in me, an anxiety
I cannot explain at all

it has to do with school
third or fourth grade elementary, we were
forty or forty-five children, the classroom
large, oblong, I sat
quite far away
the teacher far away at his lectern
Sometimes something happened to me then
which made the teacher up there shrink, be
thrown infinitely far away
in a room growing larger and larger, especially
his head
grew infinitely small, he screamed and shouted, once
he broke his pointer on
the lectern so that
one of the pieces fell beside my desk
I said nothing to anyone

In my own head a strong white light was generated
The same light
the same splitting and swinging away occurred
when first I heard
this music, 1959

~

At a desk diagonally behind me sat a large girl
who used to have fits of some kind,
she would throw back her head and arch
over her desk, I
remember it as if in utter silence, before
the rattle in the throat, the lowing sound
emerges, comes
from within myself, grows into
a scream, roars from pain and from despair

the music is full of despair
it breaks inside my head

nobody talked to her
nobody talked to me

~

Grandfather had a cancer of the throat, the silence
grew in his throat, they said
because of too much singing
It is dangerous to open your mouth

Music sings with a wide open mouth

I was often beaten in the school yard, the others
standing round me in a circle screaming
I fought, in utter silence

rocking my head, my body
feeling the tears come
infinitely long ago
infinitely old

beneath this music is the growing globe of fear
colorless or the color of brass

∼

Without my ego's momentary shadow
the world's straight current of signs
would break up and obliterate
my whole being, my body
would be wholly identical
with the world's straight, dazzling surface
small bundles of energy
which kindle irregularly, flame up
like a small vortex in empty space and time

The straight white surface sings in A-major

Mozart doesn't exist any more

Nothing exists any more

Nothing is going to exist any more

IV

Laundry Lists and Manifestoes

People often leave no record of the most critical or passionate moments of their lives. They leave laundry lists and manifestoes.

—A.S. Byatt

I am writing a manifesto and I don't want anything, I say however certain things and I am on principle against manifestoes, as I am also against principles.

—Tristan Tzara

He brought me also a box of sugar, a box of flower, a bag full of lemons, and two bottles of lime juice, and abundance of other things: But besides these, and what was a thousand times more useful to me, he brought me six clean new shirts, six very good neckcloaths, two pair of gloves, one pair of shoes, a hat, and one pair of stockings, and a very good suit of cloaths of his own, which he had worn but very little: In a word, he cloathed me from head to foot.

—Defoe, *Robinson Crusoe*

∼

Nausicaa heard a buzzing in her ear.
A whisper—Girl, you left
The laundry waiting over night. That list, where is it?
Sashes, dresses, bedspreads, sheets & socks,
Your royal father's robes . . .
Expect a manifesto any moment that may issue from
The throne—not Alcinous', but one
Much higher, darker, grander, more sublime. I may look
Like Dymas' daughter, but behold:
I bring you soap and bleach and starch from very heaven.
Take your girlfriends and your maids. Take
A beach ball too.

     Elsewhere in that meanwhile, Yahweh
Stood complaining in the water that was now
Just ankle-deep—Girl, he said to Japheth's wife, you left
The laundry waiting over night. That list, where is it?
Quick before the waters all recede and we stand here in sand:
Wash the dirty linen and the garments of them all—Japheth,
Shem and Ham, N himself & Mrs N—
Here's the soap and bleach and starch. Here's a beach ball too.
But where is Noah's manifest?

∼

N in fact had lost it, drunk inside his tent, and couldn't
Reconstruct it from his memory; all those birds and
Mice and cats and dogs and even bugs and things. It seemed
As arbitrary as a laundry list. Still, old Yahweh'd brought
Them through and wanted an accounting. He took
His own frustration out on Ham who stood outside the tent
Staring at his father's genitals. Don't stare at my genitals, said N,
And soon thereafter issued his explosive anti Canaan manifesto . . .

Meanwhile in the elsewhere, Nausicaa was playing
With her beach ball having done the wash and laid it out on
Rocks to dry: her thong, her super-low-cut jeans, her black lace
Demi-bra and other things she'd ordered from the catalogue
She read with flashlight in the night hiding underneath her sheet.
Suddenly a stranger came out of the bushes holding
Just a leafy twig to hide his genitals. She told him that her name was
Nausicaa and that she'd come to do the wash. Then
She asked to see his manifest. Alas, he said, I've lost it with
My ship and all my men, but you can put this on
Your laundry list—and took away the twig. Impressed, she
Bathed the stranger in the stream where she had washed
Her under things along with father's robes and brother's
Cricket togs. But soon she realized she'd left the list itself at home
With half the things the whisperer had spoken of.

∼

We have the record of the stranger's deeds, his wily ways,
His journey home when washed and dressed and
Celebrated at the court of Alcinous. We have the history of
Abram's offspring after Babel. But Shem and Ham and Japheth,
Gomer, Madai, Javan, Tubal, Meshech, Tiras, Riphath,
Togarmah and many others on the J & P lists might as well be
Coat and tie and shirt and trousers on the one Nausicaa left at home
That floats up on a foreign shore right now.
Of Nausicaa little else is known (though more has been
Surmised.) She went on with her wash.
Zeus & Yahweh went on to become Suprematists
(The empty squares of cities not, as Kasimir Malevich
Was to say, mere empty squares).

~

Even in Vienna they could feel the earth shake as Poseidon
Dropped a mountain in the harbor of the Phacians.
For a moment, Donna Anna ceased to sing *Come furia disperata;*
Il Commandatore dropped his guard
Just long enough to feel the sting of Giovanni's sword. As they
Resumed, the maestro lost his place & skipped to Leporello's
Laundry list: *Ogni villa, ogni borgo—*
Sing along with me yourself—in Italy six hundred eighty,
Germany two hundred twelve, France a hundred,
Spain a thousand—wenches
Maidens, ladies of the court: the laundress
Or the duchess or the barely legal teen: any shape or any age:
Nella bruna, la costanza; nella bianca, la dolcezza;
Tall or short or thin or fat, horny singles, desperate wives,
Non si picca se sia ricca se sia brutta se sia bella
Purche porti la gonnella . . .

∼

    Giovanni turns up as
A stoned guest in Zurich, Tristan Tzara thundering
Against the 1 and 2 and 3 of things
While Leporello's list of ladies finds its way to Ararat to
Be released as species in the long dream of Darwin.
But who was girl eighty-six in Germany? girl fifty-four in Italy?
Who one hundred three in Spain? Who was thin and
Who was fat, who was barely legal? Simultaneologists debate
These questions with the Paratactical Historicists.
The friends of Nausicaa were Tamar and Elvira? Zeus & Yahweh
Sang like Il Commandatore, looking on the dead at Troy
And Sodom and the Somme?
                                        Nausicaa washes on and on,
Her hands all red and gnarled. Her father wouldn't know her,
Nor would you. She washes out the blood of centuries.
Her list is endless and includes those things
You got for all but nothing at the Army-Navy store:
The shirt with corporal's stripes, a neat hole through the pocket
Right above the heart; a greatcoat out of which she never
Got the stains. The *manus* in the manifesto was cut off by Saladin,
Strictly following Koranic Law. *Profit not by Prophets*, one
Apostate's declaration had begun. *Yangtse not by Yahweh*
Sang a lost Confucian ode. Rebel Angels in a flight
Of biwing planes out of meanwhile into
Elsewhere and beyond . . .

~

For their fine linen, Chapman's Homer says, *Trojan women and*
Their fair daughters had a Laundry. Heywood: *Except the sonne shyne*
That our clothes may dry, we can do ryght nought in our wash.
Crabbe: *Fair Lucy First, the laundry's grace and pride. . . .*
And as for Lists: did Homer crib his own from sub-Mycenaean
Catalogues all full of places no one can identify & captains who arrive
In ships with fanfare out of elsewhere, never to be mentioned once again?
This was not the place where all his listeners nodded off
Or turned the dial back to classic rock. It was his great & cinematic feat
Of memory, & everybody hung on these 300 lines claiming for himself some
Otherwise unknown and well-born forebear, basher of skulls,
As the high if broken branch of their family tree. He'd take off into
It by error sometimes trying to remember what came next
In his more recent poem. In the midst of *Odyssey* the fans of *Iliad*
Would startle him by shouting out: *Do the bloody ships.*

∽

Fair Lucy First, said Crabbe. Who was Lucy Second? Or was he
Counting off a list, with Lucy first, Sally next, then Jane?
(All of them together laundry's grace and pride)
To list . . .
            incline to one side, tilt; heel over as in danger
On a stormy sea; listen as in *List, Nausicaa, you left the laundry
Over night*—or *List, Donna Anna, do it like a Furia Disperata*;
To be pleasing or to satisfy, to be disposed; n. a desire or inclination;
A narrow strip of wood; an area for tournaments, a place of combat,
Ridge thrown up between two furrows by a lister; written entry
Of particulars or people sharing things in common, as
Pêneleôs, Lôitos, Arkosilaôs, Prothoênor, and other captains,
All Boiotians: Eilésion, Erythrai, Eleôn—
                                      Or Sidon, Heth,
And others from the seed of Noah out of whom the Y god
Made his nations; or the girls
Of the Anti-Giovanni League whose manifesto was the work
Of Lucy I, executed by authorities, succeeded by
Her daughter, Lucy II, honored as a forbear in
The long awaited listserve Cyborglog.com
Good St. Wystan; Never trust a critic who does not like lists—
The genealogies in Genesis, the Catalogue of Ships.
Manifestos, meanwhile,
can be used like Manna (4): exudate of the Eurasian ash,
Fraxinus ornus, taken as a laxative
In any kind of wilderness [Aramaic, *mannā*,
Hebrew, *mān*]. There was a knight who listed for a maid,
But we are merely in the background of his great
Seduction scene, plowing furrows, sorting beans and lentils,
Coriander, wheat.

∼

Maidens, kilt your skirts and go?
Mary, I want a lyre with strings Me so oft
my fancy drew Men grew sae cauld, maids sae unkind
Methought I saw my late espousèd saint Milton!
thou shouldst be living at this hour Mine be a cot beside the hill
More love or more disdain I crave Most Holy Night
that still dost keep Mother I cannot mind my wheel Much
have I travell'd in the realms of gold
Music, when soft voices die My Damon was the first to wake
My dead love came to me and said My dear and only Love
I pray My delight and thy delight My heart
aches, and a drowsy numbness pains My heart is high above
my body full of bliss My heart is like a singing bird My heart
leaps up when I behold My little son
who look'd from thoughtful eyes My life closed twice
before its close My lute, awake!
perform the last My mother bore me in the southern wild
Mysterious Night! when our first parents knew . . .

we'd sort out seeds—beans & lentils, coriander, wheat, maids
And musics, all the Ms, the Ls, the Ps—
Marie and Psyche, you and I, Lucy one and two—
Hot and tired with heavy work, listless by the end of day.

~

Broken bits of tablet, tokens, tallies, notches,
Tabulation in cuneiform. In Tom Sawyer's pocket there are
Nouns: *fish-hooks, a lump of chalk, a marble.*
Ubi Sunt or Blazon?
Distributio, Expolitio, Incrementum: or make a mingle-mangle
Of it, or a concatenation. Congeries. Enumeratio.
Rocks, caves, lakes, fens, bogs, dens and so and so and so.
For a chance to fly, a dead rat & string to swing it on.
Rebel Angels in their biwing planes . . .
            Pierre Albert-Birot,
Blaise Cendrars, Filippo Tomasso Marinetti.
Klebnikov.
Tzara.
Antonin Artaud.

∽

        Crusoe, like Odysseus
And Noah, lost his original list, like
Ishmael was the only soul among the farers on his ship the sea released.
Coins and precious metals were no use, although in time
He counted them. One by one he inventoried items of survivor's gold.
Spirits in the guild of fraud and guile
Perforce at Pandemonium
One by one stood up in council making manifesto of their
Will: *Manifesto for an Open War.*
Manifesto for Ignoble Ease & Sloth. Manifesto for a Nether Empire
In the Flames. Manifesto for Seduction of the Ones who
Dwell in Music, Phacia, Indices, Cockaigne, & Realms of Gold.

Them did Yahweh
Hurl headlong filthy into laundries cursed by
Noah in the son of Ham whose Canaanites and neighbors
Named the spirits (former names all lost and blotted out) the likes of
Chemos and Astarte, Thammuz, Dagon, Rimmon, Isis and Osiris,
Orus, Belial, along with Ion's Greeks, the sons of
Japheth's sons (Japheth's wife still working with Nausicaa
Somewhere on the other side of 12 degrees and 18 minutes latitude:
A storm blew westward and the ship struck sand, the sea
Breaking her apart . . .

∾

   . . . bags of nails & spikes,
Screw-jack & hatchet, grindstone & musket balls &
Guns: a quantity of powder, small shot & hammock:
Top-sail rigging rope & twine a hogshead of bread.
Runlets of rum the cables and a hawser—
Salvaged in the end by swimming out & rafting back
Eleven times until the wreckage of his battered ship blew off
The sand and sank.
Floating on the flood tide, a large red ball.
And on the beach Beelzebub with Klebnikov.
Against whom hum, said one.
Him who heaved the wave? The other, *Hum who will his tune.*
A time there was when toil gave us tithing.
Teething gave us tooth to frighten toves. Timber built a threat
To talismanic tomb.
Temper well the will to wake and wend.
A landing strip was built close by the opera house, while in
The monastery Marinetti was the single scribe
Scribbling
        love of danger, energy, revolt.
Speed and the machine. A racing car. Aggression & destruction of
Academies, museums. Only war is hygiene. Hymn who can
The multicolored polyphonic tides, the vibrant nightly fervor
Of the arsenal blazing underneath electric moons.

Thus he would inflate Nausicaa's ball.

~

As for arsenals, Crusoe built his own—the warehouse or
The magazine, he called it. He tells his diary that he'd omitted from his list
The pens, ink and paper, compasses and dials he'd salvaged
From the wreck. Also charts, perspectives, books
On navigation. He had from Portugal a Popish book of prayer;
He had three English Bibles. Needle, pins and thread, a shovel
And an axe. He stored his arms and powder in the arsenal.
He built a desk. He read a Bible and he wrote,
But not like Klebnikov, whose blather near the landing strip
Annoyed him. Declaiming through a megaphone,
Klebnikov would shout: *Zaum. Mountain. Island lu lu ssob.*
Kumara.
Nicht nicht pasalam bada eschochomo.

               Crusoe
In a fever thought he saw a man descending in
A cloud—Yahweh, Zeus, Beelzebub as anthromorph?—
Who then became bright flame, who made the earth shake
When he walked upon it. His voice was terrible.
He said: *Mein Herr, sing for anything you like you wish you want.*
The ague made him thirst, so he sang: *Water.*
Waiter, menu of medicinals
           Hellebore, H. lleborus orientalis,
Berberis vulgaris, Papaver somniferum, Tamarisk, Pearl Wart,
Baldur's blood and Bryony. Mandrake root.
Kumara?
Nicht nicht pasalam bada eschochomo.
In delirium, he spat up manifestos just like Klebnikov: *Island lu lu ssob.*
Mountain. Zaum.
All of which was Manna (4): exudate of the Eurasian ash,
Fraxinus ornus, taken as a laxative
In any kind of wilderness. [Aramaic, *mannā,*

Hebrew, mān]. *Mine be a cot beside the hill
My dead love came to me and said My heart is high above
my body full of bliss My heart is like
a singing bird Mysterious night!*
when our first parents knew you'd sort out seeds
and number names.

∽

Number for example Lord Chamberlain his men & courtesans—
Banded players in a worst of times and branded
Best of teams,
                                    trams on down the Strand
Where horses draw the mighty
Quartered for the pleasure of the bull baiters
Bear baiters
Tosspots watching sly Will Sly and fat Will Kemp
Burbage Cowley Duke & Sinklo
Hemmings tosses bright red ball Nausicaa put in play to
John Grabowski Urban Shocker Combes in center
Ruth in right and Gehrig (Yankees just before the crash) first base.
Baseless claims against the *mano / manus* fundamental to their
Manifesto also hands for pleasuring the prurient the skills of
Blanche d'Antigny La Barucci Cora Pearl
Mademoiselle the Maximum Marie Duplessis Apollonie their little hands
On little balls and pricks of players bandits poets
Princes brought to practice upright just
And honorable men.

∼

Manus. Festus. Gripped by hand.
A manifest a kind of handgrasp, then a slap.
Some Cora's John in Chamberlain his men's most recent
Travesty of history, thumb and digits set to curve a little Latin o,
Hurls haptic knowledge over printer's plate
As now garroting or the axe could end the asking touch me now.

Touch me how, old clown? Some festive Feste's ball game
Play house place of ill repute? Even in the elsewhere
With their handicaps. From the handbook: bite the hand that
Feeds you eat out of another's hand & oh
Although hands down
And on the other hand lay hands on him high handedly
Throw up your hands or tip just one they're clean it's heavy
Got to hand it to you . . .
        handkerchief or handiwork
Or Nausicaa's red ball—

Manifesto of the Fully Opposable Thumb:

∼

[. . . although between ellipses & in brackets, toes
Of manifestoes must be noted too: Man the nomad,
Aboriginal, creature of the large toe
Before the thumb, may have got a toe-hold on the
Path or rural route, sung his world into
Being, exited his animal & cave through a desert
Or an outback, grown his brain beyond co-laterals,
Memorised his lines, walked from Egypt,
Walked from Chareville
—a misprint in our own recent treatise on the
Bogomils confuses *songs* and *slogs*—*Lettre du Voyant* a
Manifesto of the foot and not the hand?
Ask the Abyssinian Rimbaud if toffs at dinner back
In Trojan's Dinar Diner (pizza and kebab)
Know enough to throw a toggle switch or even
Tattoo *tau*: a young lady in my colleague's
Final class before retirement going to the dean about
His sexist language when he said she
Shouldn't pussyfoot around, prevarication not to
Be desired but also not to be confused with
Eager toe of prurient intent . . .
                                             Slog on]

∼

   . . . thumb that makes for consciousness, &
Not the other way around. Forty thousand years, more or less,
Since Chiro Adónaison uploaded agency.
No paw or claw or forefoot but the Ur-tool blessed by every
Tinker tailor soldier spy who
Once was hominid & grasped itself becoming manifestal
Agent for a span beyond biology—Anaxagoras, who
Shook the hound of Aristotle, tooling down
The highway in his supercharged Lamarck. Thumb is up or down
Or meeting digits picking up a pickled pepper
Thumb opposes fully human fall from grace and makes
With fingers ancient fist to shake against the sky. Handsome Tom
Says touch me now Apollonie she says I will
My sweet and lovely biped all because of chiro-genesis.
Chiromancy to reveal Arminians among the flock?
Manifesterians all, depravity is only partial, freedom opens
Like a chiropractor's palm.

~

Hand me down prehension goes that line of thought
Or you'll construct a Calvinist at Leiden.
Courtesans in court deny their destiny is manifest
But list their favorite tricks. Prehensile tallies where
The RBI statistics all emerge, but prehistoric to a one
The hook-grip, scissor, five-jaw chuck
The disk- & sphere- & squeeze-grip: pops it up in short left field
Where Robert Meuseul hauls it in and throws
It all the way to Gehrig catches runner well off base besides.
And who's that girl whose touch becomes professional—
Former maid of music, product of the crazy Liszt—
Handy in her knowledge of applause
When sign of wantonness and frank caress
May guarantee a patron and the reigning Traviata
Singing like a caged Macaw? In Crusoe's dream a thumb
And fingers slip into her house the night she dies
And take her tinker taylor's tintype, take her
Bird food, bracelet, banquet table, comb
And brushes, candelabrum, Bible, letters, contraceptive pills
And all the words that tell her story. They take the gifts
Nausicaa left her, all the notes she played, her
Brooklyn lover and her Dumas *fils*. They take her *aux camélias*
Her Duplessis and her Marie. They
Take her *touch me here* and *bonne nuit mes amis*

∼

Therefore, they pass by—Nausicaa and the
Demimondaine girls—with nothing to declare at customs
By the foot of Ararat except themselves
While at the summit of the world above a Sea of Boos & Outrage
He who makes the martyrs to the proposition that
Sublime is Always Now and Everything is Always the First Time
Declines in power wondering if everything is always
The last chance. In Epistemon's visit to Elysium
The riffraff out of Rabelais work on: Joyous Dr. Festus who
Was hand-gripper, hand-groper,
Puts his hands not in the bowl of cherries but in earth
Beside a grove where all the others labor too
Digging their own graves. Xerxes cries for mustard, Cyrus
For his cows; Ulysses sews a shroud while
Agamemnon washes corpses and the sons of Fabius
Thread beads . . .
      Poor Marie must sort out seeds.
Given Psyche's task, she can't tell beans
From lentils on her list, can't tell oats
From peas from Q's from qu-bits, can't find missing
Letters of the alphabet or find the cancelled tickets
For the lector's lecture on the laws . . .

～

. . . mislaid by fingers that mis-key command for mitzvah,
Change *Nausicaa's* to *Eurekas*
In a spell check: *Cyborg Manifesto* is immediately downloaded
While the courtesans gather up their reputations, enter
Through consumption in the lungs of Verdi's score: Virus has her
Way with Listserve, hands re-tool as handmaids
Of the process working on its own. Letters of the alphabet interpreted
As all the saved epistolary files, and so the poem in progress
Is sent out from A to Z. Giovanni grows prosthetic
When confronted with the simulacrum of the Dada Modest Woman,
Baroness Von Frytag-Loringhoven plus
Attachments: coal-scuttle headdress & the nipple-rings dangling
Down brass balls. Cyborg manifesto steps
Around both Zeus and Yahweh to embrace Chimera as a fabricated
Hybrid: Tools are coded stories and the copies don't
Require an original. It may cost an arm and leg, but consider
The alternative. Where medicine's a hermeneutic of the network,
Noumena become *Das Nichts*. Arrange a nano-implant and proceed
To disengage: Cyborg semiology signals to theology; God nor
Goddess may survive the creatures of an integrated circuit
Leaving laundry lists & manifests trailing from the greatest moments
Of their lives, dualisms of a hierarchy naturalized
Before the language took on fusion of the *manus* & machine
Whereby Nausicaa never wakes despite the urging of the one
Disguised as Dymus' child.

∾

Noah says *Who cares about my*
Genitals when Ham looks in his tent. Kasimir Malevich paints
Away at academic nudes; Klebnikov embraces the
Horatian ode. When Donna Anna sings *Come furia disperata*,
Il Commandatore kills her on the spot; Caruso sails
Away where 12 degrees and 18 minutes latitude's the formula
For song; Tzara praises 1 and 2 and 3.
Biplane avant guardists loop their loops in functions
So recursive there is no avant to guard, radio an
Elsewhere in the meanwhile where it's all
A mingle-mangle, concatenation. Surface now
Outfaces depth and replication reproduction as the odd
Dualisms will no longer dial up: whole/part, woman/man
Living/Dead, maker/made or courtesan or maid or player or
The played. Aacisuan and 911 and Sessylu respond
O Mussulmans, save our goods from wretched unbelievers,
Look what's in our pocket, Tom: He words us, girls,
Mechanic slave with rule and hammer, saucy lector catches
Us like strumpets, scald rhymer who extemporally enacts
Our greatness as a squeaking boy—
Fish-hook, marble, lump of chalk. O dead rat and
String to swing it on!

∼

First image ever streaming in of Monad
Claiming two hemispheres and four
Calculators for its cinema, gonad aching from a Yankee
Curve that got it in the groin: grainy movies of
The all-departing all escorted by the simulacra on their screen:
Counter tenors, sheep and goats, fallen angels, obtuse
Angles, David's armies, birds of paradise and beasts
Of the apocalypse. Clans of courtesans & baseball fans hurrah
Among the tangled wires and brachia
The polys, seriations, pleonasms in extreme
While slipping into sequence of possessive phrases
Of the quantum of the zero of the one of the watcher
Of the disambiguating
      decoherence of the end of the beginning
         and beginning of the end
Of the letter of the law of the laughter of
    the lawless . . . (1)

∼

            . . . while on a promontory broken off
The screensaver image of an ancient SE10
Madam C's nine cognates gather around boxes dropped
By Ever Afterlife Balloonists working on the script
Of *Cargo Cults*. They argue (the cognates) that a manifest
Attached to shipment listing all collaterals and cogs,
Codes and codices for Mme's Nothing Else Cockaigne Machine
In fact are elegiac poems, that David sings for Jonathan,
Gilgamesh for Enkidu. They inscribe themselves as
Manifestoes which proclaim their faith in algorithms of an
Unknown field of force. They're cognizant and they can glow.
They're coeternal, and they rise to an occasion.
Although they tell no story of their lives, their little trumpets blow.

V

Kedging in Time

[Kedge, v. intr. A. To warp a ship, or move it from one position to
another by winding in a hawser attached to a small anchor
dropped at some distance; also trans. To warp. B. Of a ship:
To move by means of kedging.] Poets, too, may cast an
anchor well before them, pulling forward when attached
to something solid, only then to cast their anchor once again.

For some of the families involved:

Drury-Lowe, Adams, Bonham-Carter, Hilton-Young, Young

Part I

Thirty-Nine Among the Sands, His Steps

or riddle there:
                    who may have sailed the Alde, and out into
the sea, but still was not the helmsman,
she was he, the captain's daughter, child too
of children's strategies on tidal rivers
where the toy wooden soldiers rose
in marshmist reeds and tipped their Bismarck helmets
to the girls, *Achtung*!

                        Cousin Erskine had preceded
by some leagues
and even Uncle Win. Sons of Lord Anchises,
prophesying war, sang
of arms and men who had come back again
by whom the bundled fasces were
restored . . .

~

or sailed in the channel all alone, the narrow sea
and north. Or with a friend to crew,
his maps about him and his nerves in perfect
order but his thoughts preoccupied
in case the Hun would launch those lighters full of infantry
from waters around Frisian islands or between
the unmapped sands and point them
toward the Wash or Suffolk shingle where no yachtsman
out of Orford, Harwich, Woodbridge or along
the Essex flats would come at them
like Jellicoe out of some dispatch he read at Scapa Flow . . .

~

or sat there with a romance, *Zenda* say, just as she
had done, and Winston doubtless too whose
own *Savrola* marked a pause between the Bores and bells
of a pugnacious dreadnaught caught in shore fire
steaming up the Dardanelles . . .

                           Fortune had to sail up the narrow
channel between heavy guns in batteries
on either side. The harbor city of Laurania could be
bombarded from the port, but only if
the ships survived their passage. *Petrarch* and *Sorato* followed,
turrets slowly turning, firing at embrasures
and the barbette mounted canons on the rocky banks.
Black smoke poured from stricken ships and
water jetted from the scuppers as emplacements pounded
the returning Admiral and his sailors who
had come from Port Said to quell rebellions in this
Ruritanian romance. He paced the quarter deck like Nelson
while Savrola waited for him with subaltern and
Antonio Molara's widow whom he loved, dreams of a
Republic in his brain . . .

~

Or simply dreams of power, he thinks,
and puts aside his pen to pour himself a gin. It is 1897.
He'll publish this in 1900 and become
First Lord in time to send his ships into another well-defended
strait. Does in fact do this and thinks of Xerxes' bridge across
the narrows and Leander's swim from Sestos,
Byron too aspiring to the Hellespont, Troy on the Asian side
and Schliemann's archaeologists in search of Bronze Age
towers now become the Kaiser's gunners when
in 1915 ships steam out of romance up the channel toward
The Marmora, *Agamemnon* and *Inflexible* bombarding Turkish
forts at Kilid Bahr, mines and shore fire blasting
Irresistible into a drifting and
abandoned hulk . . .

～

Or an abandoned plan: evacuation scuttles the agenda which
had confidently hoped to open the Aegean
once again to Russian ships and drive the Turks beyond
Constantinople by a landing
from the barges which were built on orders
to attack—not Gallipoli—but points along the German Baltic coast.
Only Richard Hannay knew that Wilhelm gave it out he was a secret
Muslim and proclaimed a Jihad in Islamic lands
against the Brits. Davies & Carruthers
sailed the *Dulcibella* through the Kiel Canal early in the century.
What they saw might well preoccupy the Admiralty
in these contentious weeks, Sea Lord
Fisher hiding at a Charing Cross hotel from Lloyd George.
Someone sends out copies of *The Riddle of the Sands*
to sailors at the Firth of Forth and Scapa Flow where only fiction
saw as early as '03 the dangers lurking in the Frisians
for the eastern coast. The real skipper of that prophecy is executed
by a firing squad for having in his pocket such a little gun
it might as well have been a toy.

∽

But *Vixen* was no toy. Nor the guns he ran on *Asgard* to the
shores of Howth that against express intention
ended in the hands of Easter's Irishmen. In Irish, English, Frisian
or Aegean waters, what's the future of the future tense?
What's propitious in the past? Passing through the present,
kedging's all you're good for
with a foot of water under you, the tide gone out, the fog so thick
you can't see lights at Norderney but enter history in spite
of that by sounding in its shallows with an oar.
While *Petrarch's turrets turned, firing at embrasures and
the barbette mounted cannons on the rocky
banks outside Laurania* whose captain put aside his pen
to pour himself another gin and daydream about power, *Vixen* in that
sea-log sanguine summer tacked its way across the Channel
to Boulogne, then to Holland & through scattered
islands off the Heligoland Bight,
Wangerooge and up the Elbe past Cuxhaven, then through
Wilhelm's ship canal into the Baltic
and the Schlei Fiord, then back . . . .

           1897's log ends up intact
in 1903's fiction that prefigures 1915's fact:
*Groped three-reefed and gale grew much worse
with heavy rain, wind veered to northeast
and blew a hurricane. Soon got into breakers found a devil of a
situation fearful work with tiller several heavy jibes
when close inshore then grounded but blew off again entire population
of the beach was waving. Dunes obscured by such high tide
but soon we tore into the mouth of something like a harbour, let go
anchor with a run then luffed and brought up just in time
with bowsprit over quayside, crowds of people standing and amazed
as if we'd fallen from the sky.*

~

In the sky, Zeppelins and buzzing biwing sea-planes.
In the epilogue, memorandum taken from a stove
in Norderny deciphered well before Room 40's codemen went to work
that indicated plans to send an infantry with light artillery
out of Frisian mists on lighters pulled by tugs of shallow draft and
land them on the flats along the Essex coast, perhaps at
Brightlingsea, perhaps the north side of the Wash.
The skipper of the *Vixen* and the riddler of the sands,
a deuce of trouble for the aces of *echt deutch*, climbs
aboard a Short 136 & flies north-east above the U-boat shoals,
navigates with maps he'd drawn of islands, channels, tides when
only fishermen and pleasure craft sailed from the mouths of
Elbe and Wesser, Ems and Jade, when no ships of the *Hochseeflotte*
hid from some definitive Trafalgar.

Part II

~

Or from the Master of the *Dulcibella*.

His official paper
for the Admiralty is called
The Seizure of Borkum and Juist. It turns
an epilogue to forward policy proposing that the barges being
shipped to the Aegean should return, that islands which
command the branches of the Ems be taken by surprise, the German
North Sea coast blockaded. *Then invade the Frisians
in a major action, mine all river mouths and sink a wall of scrap,
follow mapping made in fiction, loosing Russian allies
on the Baltic coast in fact.* Churchill & the Sea Lords choose Gallipoli.
But not before commending him for valor in the air
and prescience at sea. Easter's Ireland waits.
In villages near Lowestoft they shout *Them roundels
on the fuselage is us.* And airships drift above the sea like
great balloons escaped the clumsy hand of Albion's
last giant's giant child. Commanders at the Harwich harbor
seek to maintain what they call an "atmosphere."

Hannay's word as well: an atmosphere. But not just one of
mastery, control, intimidation on the seas, though he too seeks
a new Trafalgar when the code words *Hafgaard Luneville Avocado Pavia*
begin to yield results and *High Tide 10.17* reveals
in tables at the Admiralty a big chalk headland close to Bradgate
and the murderous Black Stone who'd steal plans for disposition
of the ships at Scapa Flow and Rosyth just by blending in so well
that ministers and brass around the council table
might take someone with a beard and heavy hooded eyes
to be Lord Alloa himself.

∼

                    Trafalgar Lodge establishes
another atmosphere in days *when wildest fictions are more probable
than facts*. No one shouts out there around the tennis lawn or in
the smoking room among those gentlemen the spies, *Them roundels
on the fuselage is us*. The fact is Hannay's Buchan worked in codes
for Captain Hall, "The Blinker"—man of penetrating heavy
hooded eyes—while Buchan's Hannay found himself employed by
Alfred Hitchcock in the run up to another war. Just ask
Mr. Memory, whose paratactic act will be the death of him
at the Palladium: *When was Crippen hanged? What's the measurements
of Miss Mae West? When was General Gordon at Khartoum?
Who swam Hellespont? What's a monoalphabetic cipher what's
sunk off the Ulster coast where's the veldcraft chap who o'er the
hill and moory dale pursues Arimaspian in Schicksalskamf? What's
the peripeteia of the anagnorisis? What's the number of steps?*

While Hannay tiptoes toward Trafalgar Lodge and notes
the tennis lawn, the marguerites, geraniums and other seaside flowers,
a yacht with Squadron's ensign rocks at anchor at
high tide. 10.17. In the Dardanelles, evacuation's under way
the day the book which he inhabits enters time.
He wonders what may melt into an atmosphere, leak out of a landscape.
Then he blows his little whistle, twice. Someone's shouting out *das Boot*,
and then *Der schwarze Stein*. The fat man who escapes becomes
Von Schwabing in another place, Hannay Hitchcock's
creature in another time. Soldiers of the Empire, reading
one another's books, might find one who flew Cuxhaven's raid
remembering at Harwich guns he ran on *Asgard* after Black Hand Serbs
had shot the Archduke, Wilhelm sailing the Norwegian
fiords in *Hohenzolleren* fully sixteen years after *Vixen's*
journey north;

~

                     twelve years after *Dulcibella* kedging
in the tidal stream; nineteen years of Isle of Wight regattas bringing
cousins Nicky, Willy, George to lunch at Osborne House,
boats from round the world to dip their pennants while the guns
saluted Kaiser, King, and Tsar . . .
But this is for the Dublin Volunteers. This is from
the men who shipped their freight from off the *Gladiator* bobbing
by the light ship north of Dover, then set mainsail,
mizzen, spinnaker and sailed toward a passage through maneuvers
of the fleet off Cowes. Near Brighton, practice firing from the
warships lights the pier where boys in shorts and girls in
pinafores stare into the west and *Asgard* sails on to Spithead,
brass bands playing on the decks of dreadnaughts passing
in review, their rails lined with sailors and marines. When the weather
turns against her, *Asgard* beats up past the Lizard, somehow
tacks around Land's End to Holyhead, then across the Irish Sea
fighting a nor'easter at full gale.

But go ask Mr. Memory: *Exactly who were Dublin Volunteers?*
Was De Valera there? Did Erskine Childers eat Carruthers' heart?
Who returned to Ireland in a German submarine when
Asgard's captain still served Empire and Ascendancy in Short 136
in skies above the Heligoland Bight? Who was hanged and who was shot
and why? Did Churchill cheer and did Cuchulain weep?
Who steps Thirty-Nine among the sands or riddles there
who also may have sailed the Alde? On 29 July the fleet leaves
Portland in the dark to pass the straits of Dover, eighteen miles of
warships undetected steaming toward the foggy empty waters
in the north . . .

∼

                     and Pamela was nine.
She lived near Rosyth in the little coastal
village, Aberdour. Her father was a captain & she sometimes
saw his ship out on patrol. She wished she were a boy
and could go to sea herself and didn't like it when
her mother & the other naval wives would say
But you can marry a sailor! Precocious reader, she'd go down
to the rocks emerging at low tide with Buchan or Childers,
Rider Haggard or Hope. She'd be the hero on the run,
she'd be the spy, she'd be the swashbuckling master
of a masked identity. Then she'd make a large uncovered stone
her ship, fire a broadside at the Germans who were hunting
through the fogs to find her father and, although
she didn't know it, her future husband too. Her own child
would also be a captain's daughter and the strategist of
tidal rivers to the south where toy wooden soldiers rose in marshmist
reeds and tipped their Bismarck helmets to the girls, *Achtung!*
Achtung! her father joked, running towards her laughing down
the iron pier where landing craft left officers and men
who now and then were granted leave. He'd walk with her along
the narrow path between the bay and village, rightful
king of Ruritania, prisoner freed from Zenda and engaged
to Princess Flavia; and she'd be Rudolph Rasyndyll
dueling for his borrowed crown & honor with Black Michael's
black usurping henchmen on the castle bridge.
Then her father's utter great fatigue would overwhelm him
and he'd lie down in the sun,
shade his aching eyes with his daughter's open book. . .

~

If you asked Mr. Memory about these two, he'd be
confused. Father, daughter? Captain, mate?
Two red-headed Rudolphs? Richard Hannay and his scout Pienaar
cloaked entirely in an atmosphere & sharing stories with
the very man who stalked them? Mr. Memory at the Palladium
might falter, but not Mrs. Adams, 94, perhaps the last alive to have
seen the things she's seen, telling ancients at the ancient public school
converted to a home: *And I was Pamela, a child, and yet I
saw it all. Every ship on the horizon steaming in formation
while the two of us would sing dispatch or distich there
beneath the sign of all these sails: darting in and out & crossing tacks
at fifteen knots, the yachtsmen heading for the Kiel Regatta,
Wayland, Nigel, Ian: Monarch firing from the
forward turret out of fog by whom the bundled fasces or
the kingdom come* She kissed her father's eyes
and read him stories from her book.

Part III

∽

Or Cousin Nicky read—
                to Grand Duchess Olga and her sisters
at the Tsarskoye Selo Palace, at Tobolsk, at Ekaterinburg.
Soon they would be shot like Easter's Irishmen
who borrowed *Asgard's* cargo for their cause when her captain tried
to reconcile the Empire & Home Rule. And he too would be shot,
eventually. And even Mr. Memory. And everything dragged on in horror
on the Western Front, and Nicky read

∼

Some comfort, maybe, that Pienaar & Hannay & their colleague
based on T.E. Lawrence got up as a Kurdish gypsy
helped to take Erzerum from the Turks despite the Kaiser's jihad
and Companions of the Rosy Hour through intelligence revealed
in actual fact by Russian deputies
on tour of Scapa Flow in February of that year.
He read how Nicholas had breached defenses with his Cossack
cavalry while he, Nicholas himself, would give
his kingdom for a horse. His daughters ask him to read on.
He is reading this in English and the guards
who never lunched at Osborne House all mock him as he says
Greenmantle is St. Francis run by Messalina.
That confused the Duchess who was thinking about
butterflies, or were they moths—Monarchs, Admirals,
Greenmantles. But Greenmantle is the Kaaba-i-Hurriyeh
for all of Islam and will wear the green ephod of prophet
for Von Einem and the Turks; they'll rise inspired to hold Erzerum
unless intelligence is taken through the lines informing
Nicholas that flanks up in the hills, west and south-west,
can be turned, for they are undefended by a single trench.
As the Russian columns move at the Euphrates' Glen,
Hannay understands that Pienaar has got through, a map inside
his shirt, and that horsemen at the gap are soldiers
of the Tsar—who reads the book, a prisoner with his daughters,
sisters of the moths and butterflies remembered from
the Isle of Wight . . .

In Room 40
Buchan keeps the watch through weeks of work
on plaintext elements and homophones in hybrid code
while Captain Hall, "the blinker" who has leant his features to
his colleague's villain with a twitch, a stare, and hooded eyes,
works beyond the *ar* & *auf* & *Krieg* of it, the *wenigen* & *werden*
all the way through steps and sands and riddles to
decode the Amadeus Telegram sufficiently to build
an atmosphere in which both Nicholas and Pamela read on
while polyphonic groups with nulls & diagraphs & single caps
for words not in Vocabulary—dates, effective numbers
and the rest—read themselves, in spite
of muddling *crypt* and *shipped*, *fiction* and *the faction*,
firmly into fractions of a plan more efficacious than
Carruthers', Hannay's, Hope's, or Roger Casement's—
Casement sending through a priest the message
No German Help while Blinker circulates through London clubs
the pages of a private diary that's sure to get him hanged.
As the Cossacks breach the Turkish lines at Erzerum, Greenmantle's
double in disguise shouts out: *Oh, well done our side*—
which Pamela's daughter will refuse to bellow at
the games mistress' bidding when a goal is scored, but which
somehow comforted the prison of the Tsar.

～

On *Vindictive*, Bryan Adams and his shipmates puzzle over
copies of that novel sent out by the Admiralty
to every ship. As code; as inspiration. While Pamela
and all the other children of the sailors in the north name the ships
that pass by Aberdour at twilight, then go off to cottage
and to bed, the man she'll marry twenty years from now prepares
to attack the guns at Zeebrugge. An atmosphere's to be
achieved. Flame throwers modified to belch black gouts of smoke,
hinged brows that lower fourteen bridges, great hooks to snag
the shore line, howitzers and pom-poms manned by the marines,
Stokes mortars all along the rail & riflemen on forecastle
and the boat deck up abaft . . .

                                              Shell-stars light the sky
as *Vindictive* steams out of
the smoke laid down by motor launches at her bow and turns
to landward while reversing engines and is held against
the mole by tugs pressing at her from the stern.
Sailors toss their hooks ashore and warning sirens blare.
Shore emplacements fire upon the landing party
leaping from the access deck to follow Adams toward
the guns beside the lighthouse—silenced when the viaduct is blown
and sinkships block an access to the sea.
Pamela is actually asleep by now,
her daughter reading downstairs by the fire. Once again
her husband rushes toward the lighthouse just like a hero
in some romance—*Good show and cushy job.*
I say, Adams, that was damned impressive
though your lads got rather rattled by machine gun fire.
If you ask next morning what the
celebration is, Mr. Memory will say Remembrance Day—
and poppies blooming red in every field.

～

But he doesn't recognize the young American walking with
the family to the little Norman church
in Hacheston. The old Captain is remembering the raid.
His wife's remembering her father and the Scottish village
near the Firth of Forth. Their daughter is wondering
if she should marry the American. There's a brief ceremony
at the cenotaph, and then the several families who have
climbed the little hill disperse . . .

                          In the afternoon
there's sailing on the Alde. The American is not much of
a sailor, but does what he is told. The river's difficult to navigate
and full of sands and bars that can catch you at low tide
and keep you for the night. They sail slowly out from Aldeburgh,
past the squat Martello tower at Sloughden, down
past Orford Ness, the castle keep and early warning
radar nets, the bird sanctuary, through the mouth of Orford Haven,
to the sea. The Captain smokes his pipe and snoozes in
the sun. His daughter is the helmsman and is much preoccupied,
though quite familiar with these waters where she's sailed
since early youth and imagined wooden soldiers popping up
in marshmist reeds and tipping Bismarck helmets to the girls.
Her mother rather likes the young American,
but she doubts her husband does. At dinner he'd been going
on about Virginia Woolf, his back against a bookcase
full of Kipling, Buchan, Hope—the Captain looking rather bored.
She's not thinking she'll outlive her whole generation
and become at 94 the last person to have seen, with a group of children
on her father's ship, the surrender of the German fleet.
They'll tape her for the BBC and air her comments on a program
called *Der Tag*.

~

Mr. Memory's remembering his job when
he worked for Mr. Hitchcock. They changed the story quite a lot,
making up his character from scratch. In 1935 the spies were
after plans for a silent airplane engine, not the disposition of the
British Fleet. As Hannay says to Madeleine, imported
from the studio into a story where she had no
part: *Of course there are no missing papers, all the information's
in the head of Mr. M,* whose friend Erskine Childers,
Republican at last, also had a head for things that lead him to
his end. *What's the riddle of the sands? What are the 39 Steps?*
Childers was shot by the Free State, De Valera's little gun found
about his person. Memory is shot by spies. No one
pays attention to the little boat sailing in a mild breeze
along the coast of Suffolk.

~

> But where is Greenmantle?
> Who's the rightful king of Ruritania? Where's Savrola got to
> with the widow of Antonio Molara?
> Why did Admiral Reuter scuttle the entire German fleet?

No one fires a warning shot across their bow.

They sight no ship on the horizon.

There's nothing flying in the sky except the gulls.

VI

The Back of the Book

... beck of the boat or a bike in the brook

Kedging in *Kedging in Time*

After the first version of this poem was published in *Chicago Review* under the title "Thirty-Nine Among the Sands, His Steps," I was invited to write, for the same journal, an account of its occasion and composition. Although it was impossible to pass up such an offer, there are always dangers that come with any experiment in self-reading. One doesn't want inadvertently to shut down any passages—a resonant word in the watery context of this poem—while opening up a lock here and there by way of some auto- and bibliographical heaving and hoing at cranks, gates, gears, and other kinds of machinery. Most of the ships in this tale are too heavy to portage; and a clogged sluice may now and then require a better trained nautical sleuth than the maker of the poem and author of these notes. Still, the essay was generally enjoyed and a number of readers have suggested that I reprint it in this book.

To begin with, the title of the poem changed after its appearance in *Chicago Review*. The first line is now just a first line, though still splicing the titles of two popular fictions of the early Twentieth Century, Erskine Childers' *The Riddle of the Sands* (1903) and John Buchan's *The Thirty-Nine Steps* (1915). The title is now *Kedging in Time*, and the printing, re-formatted to encourage a slow reading, follows the title with a modified quote from the OED and the dedication.

The addition of a dedication serves, I hope, to suggest at once that the poem is not entirely impersonal in the mix of literary and historical materials encountered by the reader following the first fourteen lines. In fact, by the end of the piece, it should become clear that an elegy for Pamela Adams, along with her forbears and some in her extended family, has emerged out of the various dissolves, re-windings and general historical parataxis of the text. Although fictional characters, historical figures, and family members keep an extended and perhaps an initially perplexing company in the piece, Pamela is at the center and draws the others together as daughter and wife of sailors, reader of Childers, Buchan, Anthony Hope and Ridar Haggard, writer of memoirs, step-mother, mother, mother-in-law, cousin and friend of those many members of "families involved." Although it's going to sound like name-dropping, a bit of family history may help to open up the poem.

At some point in the fall of 1966 I found myself at a party in London talking to the most beautiful woman in England. Reader, I married her. But not for a year or so. I was inconveniently married to someone else at the moment and, of course, I had to meet Ms. Diana Adams' family. That very night I made a start at what was a very long process. At the end of the party Ms. Adams suggested dropping back to "my sister's place," what I assumed would be a student flat. Her sister's name, "Liz Young," sounded reassuring enough, but my London roommate (my American wife was at Stanford), drove the four of us—the fourth was a friend who had met Liz's husband, Wayland, at I.U. in Bloomington, and *that* sounded downright Hoosier—straight up Bayswater Rd. to a private house amid hotels and high rises more or less across from the Round Pond in Hyde Park. I still thought the "student flat" might be at the back or maybe in the attic, but became a little alarmed when I saw a blue plaque near the door saying that James Barrie had written *Peter Pan* inside. Liz and Wayland lived, along with their five children, in the whole house, not just in part of it. After I got to know Wayland I sometimes thought he, with all his polymath's enthusiasms, might *be* Peter Pan.

It was quite late and all children save the eldest—that was Easter, eighteen—were in bed. After a while Wayland, and a little later Liz, came down from wherever they had been upstairs. The backdrop to a sherry and a couple of hours conversation was a large library, art on the walls by some artists I recognized—Duncan Grant in his Matisse phase, for example—and both a piano and harpsichord. As Wayland talked a little shop, it turned out that he was a member of the Wilson government and had another name—Lord Kennet.. (His paper trail is hard to follow as he's published books under the names Wayland Hilton-Young, Wayland Young, and Wayland Kennet. The changes of name suggest an intellectual restlessness that has been part of his character.) Liz, as it turned out, was Diana's half sister, daughter not of Pamela, but of Bryan Adams' first wife, Audrey, who had drowned in a swimming accident. Liz was a poet, a published authority on arms control, and co-author, with Wayland, of books ranging in subject from old London churches to Northern Lazio in Italy. On the literary side of things, they were friends of people like Wole Soyinka and William Golding; on the political side, they entertained ministers, ambassadors, and a range of high-flying academics including a man I met later that year called Henry Kissinger. Liz and Wayland were about forty. Diana was twenty-one. I was twenty-four and felt like an American pilgrim out of Henry James.

Diana had been living at Liz and Wayland's house while attending Russian classes at what was then called Holborn College. And she had lived there before, when she was doing A-levels at Queens. It must have been a heady environment for a teenage girl. Her own home was in the tiny village of Hacheston, in Suffolk, where her father had retired after serving in two World Wars. He was over eighty. Pamela was twenty years younger. They had met at the League of Nations before the Second War. Captain Adams had been pleased when his first daughter married the son of an old shipmate, Edward Hilton Young. They had served together on *Vindictive*, about which Hilton Young wrote in his book *By Land and Sea*. (It is my main source for the attack at Zeebrugge.) The Captain had been pleased enough with Wayland's early books, but didn't like his famous contribution to the zeitgeist of the 60s, *Eros Denied*. "All about sex," he sniffed when I mentioned it some years later. (It was research at the Kinsey Institute that had led Wayland briefly to Bloomington.)

Though Edward Hilton Young had proposed to Virginia Woolf in a punt on the Cam, he eventually married the widow of Captain Scott of the Antarctic. So Lady Scott was Wayland's mother. She was a sculptor and a friend of T.E. Lawrence, who sat to her for a bust. I eventually imagined both a polar waste and a desert at opposite ends of the house: one the province of Scott, the other of Lawrence. Wayland would sometimes dress up in Lawrence's Arab robes (somehow in his possession) and dash about the house with his dagger. His daughter, Louisa, writes her grandmother's life in *A Great Task of Happiness*. Another daughter, Emily, is a sculptor, like Lady Scott—and perhaps the finest living stone carver in the tradition of Gaudier-Brezska, Eric Gill, and Mestrovic.

The Scott, Young and Adams families are all from Naval backgrounds. Louisa writes in her biography that the Youngs "came from a line of runaway cabin boys and pirates which developed into Admirals." I have in my library the midshipman's log book composed by Sidney Drury-Lowe, Pamela Adams' father, from the time he was thirteen. No runaway or pirate, he came from a branch of the family which one associates with the poetry of John Donne. He, too, "developed into" an Admiral. Bryan Adams, born in Australia, also went to sea at an early age. Along with Hilton Young, he served under Sir Roger Keyes at certain points in the First World War. Thoby Young, Diana's ten-year-old nephew when I met him, eventually married Roger Keyes' granddaughter.

"And Pamela was nine." The passage that introduces Pamela to the poem finds her "near Rosyth in the little coastal / village, Aberdour." Here she waits for her father's occasional visits, reading Hope, Buchan and Childers, playing games, looking out to sea where the naval war is in progress. Part II of the poem concludes looking forward to her 94th year and her memories of the Kiel Regatta, the wartime patrols of destroyers and dreadnaughts, and eventually the surrender and scuttling of the German fleet. At the end of her life, she thought she was the last to have seen *Der Tag*, The Surrender. Her father had seen to it that she and a few other children of officers were taken out in a launch as the German ships steamed past. She tells the story in one of her unpublished memoirs, *The Iron Pier*, which is a source for this part of the poem. Out at sea her future husband was also aboard his ship. She wouldn't marry him for twenty years, but there he was. Like Pamela herself, and like her father, he had a copy of Childers' *Riddle of the Sands*. Churchill had sent copies to all ships at sea after Childers' participation in The Cuxhaven Raid in December, 1914— a raid that depended on the observations of shores, islands, canals, sandbanks, tides and military strategies of a fictional character living in a novel.

"On Vindictive . . . nothing flying in the sky except the gulls." At the end of Part III, the poem returns to Pamela by way of Bryan Adams' and Hilton Young's participation in the attack on the guns at Zeebrugge. The strategic importance of the raid would take too long to explain here, but it's worth saying that it was a nearly suicidal assignment for those, led by Captain Adams, who dashed from their ship in a land attack against the lighthouse on the mole. (Maps of the coastline from Dunkirk north to Borkum and Cuxhaven can be found in Robert Massie's history, *Castles of Steel*.) Adams survived intact while Hilton Young, still on *Vindictive*, lost an arm to enemy fire. The narrative passage describing the attack merges in the text with Pamela's half-dreaming memories on the early morning of Remembrance Day, 1966. This was my first visit to Hacheston, and there I am, "the young

American / walking with the family to the little Norman church." By the time I wrote this passage, Pamela was dead. Or, perhaps, I was writing it as she died. It is rather uncanny. Diana had flown to England in February of 2005 and had been there for a month or so, nursing her mother. The poem turned biographical and elegiac during that period. The remembered events included the Remembrance Day celebration, a first meeting between "the young American" and Pamela and Bryan Adams, pleasure sailing on the Alde, a dinner, and some awkward literary conversation in which the American tries to talk about Virginia Woolf—he was reading *Jacob's Room* coming up on the train—when the Captain said (the poem only has him "looking rather bored"): "Perhaps we've had enough of *her*," maybe referring to his future son-in-law's blather, or maybe to his own memories of his shipmate's infatuation with Virginia Woolf herself. The bookshelves there in Hacheston held some serious literature—complete sets of Hardy, Austin, Scott—but it's the talismanic Kipling, Buchan, and Hope toward whose books, unfortunately, the American has his back. As for Childers, he finally read *The Riddle of the Sands* when it was urged on him by, of all people, Geoffrey Hill.

The poem ends—aside from Mr Memory's interjection, about which more in a moment—where it began, with sailing on the Alde. I had placed "Wayland, Nigel, and Ian" in the yacht at the Kiel Regatta—an actual yachtsman, a Bonham-Carter cousin, and my newborn grandson—while of course the little sailing boat in the Suffolk river contains the Captain, his wife, his daughter and the troublesome American. Diana "sailed the Alde" quite early in life and her head was full of sometimes frightening fantasies—"children's strategies on tidal rivers / where the toy wooden soldiers rose / in marshmist reeds and tipped their Bismarck helmets / to the girls, *Achtung!*" The rest of the opening passage, however, introduces an altogether different strand of the poem:

>   Cousin Erskine had preceded
> by some leagues
> and even uncle win. sons of lord anchises,
> prophesying war, sang of arms and men who had come back again
> *by whom the bundled fasces were restored* . . .

Biographically speaking, there is no Uncle Win or Cousin Erskine in the Adams, Young, or Drury-Lowe clans. The references are to Childers and Churchill, who "had preceded" the principal family members of the poem into historical waters—and in the wake of Aeneas and Lucius Junius Brutus. Early on, Childers—an enthusiastic combatant in the Boer War—was as bullish an Imperialist as Churchill himself, and the "bundled fasces" resonate equally of Imperial Britain, Augustan Rome, Bismarck's Germany, and the Italy of Mussolini.

To compound the fiction braided at the outset around biography, Childers, as far as I know, never sailed from the Alde in Suffolk on any of his pre-World War I explorations of the Frisian islands, the coasts of Holland and Germany, and the Baltic that provided material for *The Riddle of the Sands* and, eventually, his official paper for the Admiralty, *The Seizure of Borkum and Juist*. He sailed out the mouth of the Thames. However, his journey on *Vixen*, and the journey of his characters Davies and Carruthers on *Dulcibella*, enter the poem at once as fiction and fact. Sailing *Vixen*, Childers carried with him and read Book Six of *The Aeneid* and Anthony Hope's *Rupert of Hentzau*, sequel to *The Prisoner of Zenda*. Pamela would also be reading Hope—as would Churchill.

The mapping of Davies and Carruthers, their discovery of German military secrets, and the epilogue by "the editor" dealing with the deciphered memorandum Carruthers pulls from a stove at Norderney, became a matter of great interest at the War Office after *The Riddle of the Sands* was published in 1903. Fictional characters began at that point their instruction of statesmen, Admirals, and Generals who continued listening up to and beyond the Cuxhaven Raid of December, 1914. From the first page of the poem, fictional characters move in the same world as men and women like Bryan and Pamela Adams, Hilton Young, Sidney Drury-Lowe, John Buchan, Kaiser Wilhelm, Tsar Nicholas and Childers himself.

The next several pages of text, following introduction of motifs in the initial fifteen lines, braid together Childers' articulated fear that Germany could easily launch an invasion of Britain from the Frisian islands with Churchill's reading of *The Prisoner of Zenda* and his composition of *Savrola*, the Ruritanian romance he wrote in 1897 and published first in *MacMillan's Magazine* and then, in 1900, as a novel with Hodder and Stoughton's "Sevenpenny Library." Unlike *The Riddle of the Sands*, *Savrola* would be of no importance at all if it weren't by Churchill. Written in the wake of *Zenda's* extreme popularity and between Malakand and the River War when its author was twenty-four, *Savorola* is dedicated to "The Officers of the IVth (Queen's Own) Hussars in whose company the author happily served for four happy years." In the poem, the adventures of the republican Savrola as he battles in fictional "Laurania" with dictator Morala on the right and radical Kreutz on the left, merge with an account of the actual attack at Kalid Bahr in the Bosphorus. While Laurania's fleet is recalled from Port Said to quell Savrola's rebellion—*Fortune*, *Petrarch* and *Sorato* exchanging fire with shore batteries as they attempt to gain access to Laurania's major harbor—*Agamemnon*, *Inflexible* and *Irresistible* encountered in fact a similar situation steaming up the strait to the Hellespont in the Dardanelles campaign that sent the novelist who had become First Lord of the Admiralty plummeting into temporary obscurity. Edmund Wilson said that in some ways Churchill's career gave him the impression of a person living perpetually in a boy's adventure story; the same might be said of Childers. In the case of both, their fictions prefigure events in the First War and after. And Churchill knew his Childers well. Carruthers' fear of a German attack from the Frisians became Childers' memorandum recommending a British attack from Borkum and Juist, supported by the Russians in the Baltic. Churchill chose the Dardanelles and disaster. Who knows what might have happened at Borkum and Juist?

    As Morala and Churchill "dream of power" and Churchill pauses in his 1897 composition, the poem's clock is re-set for 1915 and Gallipoli. If only the fictional Carruthers saw the dangers of a German invasion of the eastern coast of Britain from the Frisians (British barges now diverted from the Baltic to the Dardanelles), it was Richard Hannay, John Buchan's hero in *The Thirty-Nine Steps* (1915), *Greenmantle* (1916), and two subsequent novels, who knows that Kaiser Wilhelm "gave it out he was a secret / Muslim and proclaimed a Jihad in Islamic lands / against the Brits." From this point to the end of Part I, Buchan and his fictions become a new strand in the braiding, anticipating a transition from the British failure against the Turks and Germans at Gallipoli to the success of Brits and Russians—aided by T.E. Lawrence, who may be the model for Sandy Arbuthnot in *Greenmantle*—at Erzerum. As he wrote his novels, Buchan, who worked (sometimes with Lawrence) in intelligence and decoding, also wrote the ongoing chronicle (verging on propaganda) that became *The Nelson History of the War*. The strange story about the Kaiser's feigned conversion to Islam is evidently true, as it is told in the history as well as the fiction. The poem continues with the first references to Childers' adventure running guns to Ireland on the *Asgard*—guns which, though intended for the Dublin Volunteers, were eventually taken by the Irish Republican Brotherhood and used in the Easter Rebellion. While Childers was at sea, Austria sent its ultimatum to Serbia. The war began, and Childers returned to England to fly as navigator in a Short 136 pointing out details from the maps made in his head sailing *Vixen* back in 1897. Because of that, "1903's fiction [does indeed, drawing on *Vixen's* log] prefigure 1915's fact." Childers spent the rest of his life trying to reconcile his commitment to the cause of Ireland with his loyalty to the Empire. In the end, of course, that couldn't be done.

How do these and other texts function in the poem? As secure holds for the kedge-anchor of my reefed verbal craft. When I first read *The Riddle of the Sands*, I had to look up "kedge" and "kedging" in the OED. In seconds I had on my screen just the kind of list I like—*kechel, Kechua, keckle, kecksy, keddah, kedje, kedge-anchor, kedger, kedging, kedjeway*—and immediately wrote a short poem bouncing phrases off these K's. ("K,K,K, Katie" sang the Tommies and the sailors shipped to foreign ports.) The phrases include some that find their way into the present, longer poem when its poetics, as it were, is made plain:

> . . . what's the future of the future tense?
> what's propitious in the past? Passing through the present
> kedging's all you're good for
> with a foot of water under you, the tide gone out, the fog so thick
> you can't see lights at Norderney but enter history in spite
> of that by sounding in its shallows with an oar.

In the end, I thought an epigraph could make this even plainer.

The "young American" of Part III bores the Captain by going on at dinner about Virginia Woolf. I've mentioned that he was "in fact" reading *Jacob's Room*. (By 1922, when Woolf's novel was published in the same year as *The Waste Land*, modernism had begun making fiction like Buchan's look even more unsophisticated and jingoistic than it is.) In

Jacob's Room, Jacob and his friend Timothy Durrant sail from Falmouth to St. Ives Bay before the war, following the same route around Land's End that Childers took in *Asgard* in July, 1914. *Asgard*, indeed, sailed with its load of guns right through massive exercises of the British fleet which occurred at the same time, George V observing from a dreadnought. Jacob, like the characters in *Greenmantle*, travels eventually to Turkey before he is ground up in the gears of war and becomes a casualty in a world that came into being, while, as Woolf has it, "A voice kept remarking that Prime Ministers and Viceroys spoke in the Reichstag; entered Lahore; said that the Emperor traveled; in Milan they rioted; said there were rumours in Vienna; said that the Ambassador at Constantinople had audience with the Sultan; the fleet was at Gibraltar."

The fleet would be at Scapa Flow. The conclusion of Part II quotes a passage from Childers' *Vixen* log and finds Wilhelm sailing in the Baltic just before the outbreak of war. He had always envied the Royal Navy and participated enthusiastically with those other heirs of Queen Victoria, cousins Nicholas II and George V, in the parties and regattas held at Osborne House on the Isle of Wight. Admiral Jellicoe brought 150 British ships down into the North Sea to support the Cuxhaven Raid. Zeppelins and submarines ventured out, but not the great ships of Wilhelm's *Hochseeflotte*, which were hiding in the estuaries and rivers known so well to Childers. The raid achieved little and, subsequent to that, the Germans would not be drawn. There would be no early Trafalgar. There would be no Trafalgar at all, even at Jutland.

I need only identify two or three more texts—though one is a film—into which the kedge-anchor digs in order to haul this contraption forward (winds and retreating tide also sometimes pushing it back). The film is Alfred Hitchcock's version of Buchan's *The Thirty-Nine Steps*. While Part II of the poem begins with a quote from Childers' paper on Borkum and Juist and an evocation of the response in East Anglian coastal towns to seeing aircraft and ships of war, a central figure called "Mr. Memory" is soon introduced. There is no such character in Buchan's novel. He is added by Hitchcock to the 1935 film along with a love-interest for Hannay. (The latter's name is Pamela, but because of the more important Pamela in the poem, references to this character use the name of the actress who played her, Madeleine Carroll.) While ships in the North Sea, Hannay in *The Thirty-Nine Steps*,

Buchan in Room 40 (working on codes, like his hero), and the secret agents of Black Stone all try either to establish or penetrate an "atmosphere," the aim of Buchan's villains to acquire intelligence about the disposition of the British fleet becomes, once "Buchan's Hannay" morphs into "Hannay's Buchan" in the film, a search for secret plans to build a silent aircraft engine. Mr. Memory, whose music hall act involves his ability to recall an infinite number of unrelated facts when questioned by members of the audience, substitutes for Hannay's codebreaking in the novel. At the end of the film, Mr. Memory begins to reveal the secret formulas in a Palladium performance and is immediately shot. Hannay has shouted out, "What are the 39 Steps?" Mr. Memory, evidently programmed in some way to carry all the information in his head and deliver it to the villains, says "The 39 Steps is an organization of spies collecting information on behalf..." Which is as far as he gets. But the 39 Steps in the novel is a set of stairs down to the sea where full tide occurs at 10.17. At that time, Hannay finds the villains at Trafalgar Lodge—with its 39 steps—where, in the poem as well as the novel, he accosts them. He has decoded his information and followed his clues to this place and time, which is not performance time at the Palladium. "The day [when] the book which [Hannay] inhabits enters time"—publication day in 1915—happens to be a day when the evacuation was under way at Gallipoli. Mr. Memory is not asked in the poem about that, or indeed about what he happens to be doing in a poem in the first place. But he becomes the most important single figure other than Pamela. The questions that are put to him derive either directly from Hitchcock or from kedging activities already introduced. By the end of the poem he has run out of answers and, like Erskine Childers, has been shot.

Which does not mean that the reader will be unable to answer questions for him. *Did Erskine Childers eat Carruthers' / heart?* Yes. *Who returned to Ireland in a German submarine when / Asgard's captain still served Empire and Ascendancy in Short 136 / In skies above the Heligoland Bight?* That was Roger Casement. *Who was hanged and who was shot / and why?* Childers was shot, Roger Casement was hanged. For carrying an illegal weapon. For treason against the crown. *Did Churchill cheer and did Cuhulain weep?* Yes. *Who steps thirty-nine among the sands or riddles there / who also may have sailed the Alde?* Erskine Childers, Edward Hilton Young,

Bryan Adams, Diana Adams, a visiting American who'd just read *Jacob's Room*, and Pamela both old and young.

> On 29 July the fleet leaves
> Portland in the dark to pass the straits of Dover, eighteen miles
> of warships steaming toward the foggy empty waters
> in the north . . .
> and Pamela was nine.

We have now again reached the family memoir section of the poem, the long run of lines about Pamela and her father ending with their playing the parts of characters from *The Prisoner of Zenda*. Mr. Memory falters while Mrs. Adams, ninety-four, remembers; the child Pamela reads her romance to the exhausted Captain Drury-Lowe.

At the beginning of section III, "Cousin Nicky"—Tsar Nicholas II—also reads to comfort the frightened and exhausted. Amazingly, he actually read Buchan's *Greenmantle* to his imprisoned family before their execution, finding information in it Buchan got about the strategies leading to the Russian cavalry attack at Erzerum from some visiting Russian journalists, including Vladimir Nabokov's father, whom he had shown around Scapa Flow in February, 1916. Buchan wrote to his mother in October, 1917: "I saw a letter from the Grand Duchess Olga saying that she and her sisters and Papa had been greatly cheered and comforted in their exile by *Greenmantle*. It is an odd fate for me to cheer the prison of the Tsar." The narrative of *Greenmantle* is twined around Pamela's story and that of Buchan's work on codes in Room 40, details of which fascinating operations derive from a masterful source I've used off and on ever since I wrote *Pages* in 1995, David Kahn's remarkable *The Codebreakers: The Story of Secret Writing*. Surprisingly, Buchan gave the characteristic stare of Admiral Hall, head of decrypting in Room 40 and known as "Blinker" because of a twitch that accompanied the stare, to one of the villains in *The Thirty-Nine Steps*.

For the rest, the poem kedges on by way of its fictions and facts—many of the latter opened up by another masterpiece, Robert K. Massie's *Castles of Steel*—toward Zeebrugge and *Vindictive*—Hilton Young's account of Bryan Adams' landing party. When this attack occurred, Pamela was still in Aberdour, still only nine, though she would marry Bryan Adams in the end. On Remembrance Day, 1966, she must have been younger than I am now. Strange to think I'm sixty four. I wonder what she made of me. I'm sure Captain Adams knew I'd come to take his daughter away. What a loss, for me, that I was really still too young to speak to him sympathetically about his participation in two World Wars and a long life at sea. He could have told me, a sedentary grad student, much I had to learn from books for thirty years. He was by then quite deaf. Almost the first thing he said to me was that he wished the Brits were fighting with us there in Viet Nam. For a 1960s peace activist, that made things quite awkward. At lunch that day in 1966 there was a British Foreign Service type whose father had been a Commander and who had an upper lip so stiff that you could pluck it. "I do like Richard Palmer," said the Captain as my rival left the table under which Diana had been kicking me. Soon enough I did in fact take the Captain's daughter away to America and, shortly after that, he died. Pamela lived on for years, and for years we spent our summers at her house there in Suffolk. My favorite response to this poem came from one of its first readers: "I like Pamela," he said. He is not alone. She had a kind of goodness that everyone who met her felt; a Christian would say she was touched by grace, but that would have embarrassed her terribly. Her house was a kind of Howards End, and she was a kind of Mrs. Wilcox. Any lonely waif might be invited there, and many were. She outlived everyone in her generation; she even outlives Mr. Memory in the poem.

Liz and Wayland are now in their eighties and I've literally lost count of the numbers of grandchildren and great-grandchildren there are. Their magical house on Bayswater Rd., Peter Pan at the door and Lady Scott's studio at the back, still holds its magnificent past, though one wonders when the future will arrive with a wrecking ball and hotel. In the sixties, an Indian journalist called Abu Abraham lived in the studio. He once told me about his elementary education in New Delhi and a British history teacher who lectured them on what he claimed was the most important factor in the modern world since the eighteenth century. It was something that Abu wasn't quite able to get, and he wrote down "British Seepa" in his notes. British sea power.

Because of certain medical problems and an accompanying claustrophobia, I never go to England any more. For many years I was adopted by a family and conscripted (willingly enough) by a history not my own. I owe them a lot. I owe them at the very least a poem.

Notes

Sources: *Laundry Lists and Manifestoes*

Homer, *The Odyssey*, Trans. Robert Fagles; Stephen Mitchell, *Genesis: A New Translation;* Harold Bloom and David Rosenberg, *The Book of J;* Kasimir Malevich, *Suprematism;* Lorenzo da Ponte, *Don Giovanni* (the libretto); Daniel Defoe, *Robinson Crusoe;* John Milton, *Paradise Lost; Oxford English Dictionary;* Arthur Quiller-Couch, *The New Oxford Book of English Verse;* Robert E. Belknap, *The List: The Uses and Pleasures of Cataloguing;* Pierre Albert-Birot, *Banality;* Pierre Albert-Birot, *Nunism;* Blaise Cendrars, *The ABCs of Cinema;* Robert Delaunay, *Simultaneism in Contemporary Modern Art, Painting, Poetry;* Robert Delaunay, *Light,* Filippo Tomasso Marinetti, *The Founding Manifesto of Futurism;* Velimir Khlebnikov, *Selected Poems,* Trans. Paul Schmidt; Tristan Tzara, *Dada Manifesto;* Antonin Artaud, *The Theatre of Cruelty;* Antonin Artaud, *Revolt Against Poetry;* Else Von Freytag-Loringhoven, *The Modest Woman;* Mina Loy, *Auto-Facial-Construction;* Valentine de Saint-Point, *Manifesto of Futurist Woman;* Valentine de Saint-Point, *Futurist Manifesto of Lust;* William Shakespeare, *Antony and Cleopatra;* Peter Ackroyd, *Shakespeare: The Biography;* Joanna Richardson, *The Courtesans;* Raymond Tallis, *The Hand: A Philosophical Inquiry into Human Being;* Donna Haraway, *A Cyborg Manifesto: Science, Technology and Socialist-Feminism in the Late Twentieth Century;* Francis Spufford, ed., *The Chatto Book of Cabbages and Kings;* Mary Ann Caws, ed., *Manifesto: A Century of Isms;* George B. Dyson, *Darwin Among the Machines: The Evolution of Global Intelligence;* Ray Kurzweil, *The Age of Spiritual Machines;* Michèle Mètail, *1,000 Possessive Phrases.*

Endnote: *Laundry Lists and Manifestoes*

1.
9842: . . . *of the decoherence of the kedging . . .*

9843: of the quantum of the zero of the one of the watcher
of the disambiguating of the decoherence
9844: of the end of the quantum of the zero of the one
of the watcher of the disambiguating
9845: of the beginning of the end of the quantum of the zero
of the one of the watcher
9846: of the law of the beginning of the end of the quantum
of the zero of the one
9847: of the laughter of the law of the begining of the end
of the quantum of the zero

9848: of the loop of the laughter of the law of the beginning
of the end of the quantum

9849: of the player of the loop of the laughter of the law
of the beginning of the end
9850: of the rat of the player of the loop of the laughter
of the law of the beginning
9851: of the guard of the rat of the player of the loop
of the laughter of the law
9852: of the dial of the guard of the rat of the player
of the loop of the laughter

9853: of the language of the dial of the guard of the rat
of the player of the loop
9854: of the surface of the language of the dial of the guard
of the rat of the player
9855: of the depth of the surface of the language of the dial
of the guard of the rat
9856: of the groin of the depth of the surface of the language
of the dial of the guard
9857: of the tool of the groin of the depth of the surface
of the language of the dial

9858: of the virus of the tool of the groin of the depth
of the surface of the language
9859: of the hand of the virus of the tool of the groin
of the depth of the surface
9860: of the foot of the hand of the virus of the tool
of the groin of the depth
9861: of the squeeze of the foot of the hand of the virus
of the tool of the groin
9862: of the toe of the squeeze of the foot of the hand
of the virus of the tool

9863: of the sock of the toe of the squeeze of the foot
of the hand of the virus
9864: of the spy of the sock of the toe of the squeeze
of the foot of the hand
9865: of the queen of the spy of the sock of the toe
of the squeeze of the foot
9866: of the goods of the queen of the spy of the sock
of the toe of the squeeze
9867: of the scald of the goods of the queen of the spy
of the sock of the toe

[1–9842, 9868–1,000: elsewhere:
*and the appropriation of the spirit of the letter
of the kedging of the text*]

Sources: *Kedging in Time*

History: Robert K. Massie, *Castles of Steel18*; E. Keble Chatterton, *The Konigsberg Adventure*; David Kahn, *The Codebreakers*; W.G. Arnott, *Alde Estuary*. Memoirs: E. Hilton Young, *By Sea and Land*; Pamela J. Adams, *The Iron Pier* (unpublished); S.R. Drury-Low, Midshipman, *Log Book* (unpublished). Biograhy: Burke Wilkinson, *The Zeal of the Convert: The Life of Erskine Childers*; Tom Cox, *Damned Englishman: A Study of Erskine Childers*; Jim Ring, *Erskine Childers*; Andrew Boyle, *The Riddle of Erskine Childers*; Andrew Lawnie, *John Buchan: The Presbyterian Cavalier*. Fiction: Winston Churchill, *Savrola*; Anthony Hope, *The Prisoner of Zenda*; Erskine Childers, *The Riddle of the Sands*; John Buchan, *The Thirty-Nine Steps, Greenmantle, Mr. Standfast*. Criticism: John G. Cawelti and Bruce A. Rosenberg, *The Spy Story*; Mark Glancy, *The 39 Steps*. Film: Alfred Hitchcock, *The 39 Steps*. Reference: *Oxford English Dictionary*; *Rand McNally World Atlas* (Imperial Edition). Poetry: Virgil, *The Aeneid*, translated by Robert Fitzgerald.

Printed in the United Kingdom
by Lightning Source UK Ltd.
124540UK00001B/463-480/A